VRIJSTATIA

VRIJSTATIA

1. Sophie Leviseur: Memories

2. Frantz Balfet: Samuel Rolland (1801–1873), pionier van die sending in die Vrystaat

3. J.G. Fraser & James Briggs: Sotho War diaries, 1864–1865

4. Die Huis van die Armes: die Berlynse sendinggenootskap in die O.V.S., 1833–1869

5. Maude Bidwell: Pen Pictures of the Past

6. The Free State Mission: The Work the Anglican Church in the O.F.S., 1863–1883

7. Die Herinneringe van J.C. de Waal

8. The Recollections of Elizabeth Rolland (1803–1901)

9. The Bloemfontein Diary of Lieut. W.J. St John, 1852–1853

10. The Early Days of the Orange Free State

11. The Wesleyan Mission in the Orange Free State, 1833–1854

12. The Missionary Letters of Gottlob Schreiner, 1837–1846

13. The British Presence in the Transorange, 1845–1854

14. Early White Travellers in the Transgariep, 1819–1840

15. The Griqua mission at Philippolis, 1822–1837

THE GRIQUA MISSION AT PHILIPPOLIS, 1822–1837

compiled and edited by
KAREL SCHOEMAN

PROTEA BOOK HOUSE
PRETORIA
2005

The Griqua mission at Philippolis, 1822–1837
Karel Schoeman

First edition, first impression 2005

Protea Book House
PO Box 35110, Menlo Park, 0102
protea@intekom.co.za

Front cover: "Phillipolis [*sic*]" (detail)—
the mission station of Philippolis from the south-west,
with the church building just visible on the extreme left,
as sketched by James Backhouse in 1839;
from his *Narrative of a visit to the Mauritius and South Africa* (1844).

Typography and design by HOND BK
Reproduction by PrePress Images
Printed and bound by ABC Press

ISBN 1-86919-017-3

© 2005 Karel Schoeman
© All rights reserved.
No part of this book may be reproduced in any form,
without prior permission in writing from the publisher.

Prefatory Note to
Vrijstatia 14 and *15*

The Vrijstatia series was never a profitable venture from a financial point of view, and a subsidy was required for the publication of each volume. After the appearance of *The British presence in the Transorange, 1845–1854* as Vrijstatia 13 in 1992, it proved impossible to obtain subsidies for further publications, and no more work was therefore done on the three volumes awaiting publication at the time. Only now has it become possible for two of these, *Early white travellers in the Transgariep, 1819–1840* and *The Griqua mission at Philippolis, 1822–1837*, to appear in print; research materials for the third, originally projected as the journal of the Wesleyan missionary James Cameron, will be deposited with the Free State Archives Repository, Bloemfontein.

In preparing these two volumes for publication after a considerable interval, I have been unable to do more than complete the work left unfinished eight or nine years ago as best I could in my present circumstances, as my final contribution to Free State historiography. I have done no noteworthy further research myself, and have not taken into account any publications that may have appeared in the interim, apart from those for which happen to be known to me through my own involvement. As the limited pictorial records of the period have already been used repeatedly, in earlier volumes of this series as well as elsewhere, it has furthermore been decided to dispense with illustrations in these two books.

At a time when the future of the series appeared to be more promising, a number of other texts were being considered for publication, the most considerable of these being the letter book of A.H. Bain and the reminiscences of T.A. Montgomery, both in the Free State Archives Repository, the letters of young Dominee Andrew Murray from Bloemfontein, now in the N.G. Kerkargief, Stellenbosch, a selection from the correspondence of the French missionaries in the Caledon River valley, conveniently accessible in a microfilm edition published by IDC, and an anthology of contemporary accounts of the Sotho-Free State Wars. In the meantime, however, my life of active research has come to an end, and with the publication of these two volumes the Vrijstatia series must also be regarded as closed. The work I have done on it has given me much pleasure, and I trust that the published titles will continue to be of use to the historian and of interest to the general reader.

I am grateful to Human & Rousseau for their willingness to publish the series on its inception in 1982, and to the various firms and individuals who made the publication of individual volumes possible. I am likewise grateful to Nicol Stassen of Protea Book House for now undertaking to make available the remaining titles, and to Mark Ingle of Philippolis for his interest in the project and his help. As regards the final editing of the present volume, I am pleased to acknowledge the most obliging and competent help received from Marius Fortune of the Special Collections Department, National Library, Cape Town, as well as Elsa Steyn of the Africana Collection, University of the Free State, and the Free State Archives Repository, Bloemfontein.

23 February 2005   Karel Schoeman

Contents

Abbreviations and notes, *8*

1. Jan Goeyman—James Clark (1822–1827), *9*
2. The Griquas at Philippolis (1826), *22*
3. John Melvill (1827–1831), *36*
4. G.A. Kolbe (1831–1836), *65*
5. Theophilus Atkinson (1836–1840), *106*

Chronology, *127*
Suggested further reading, *131*
Index, *133*

Abbreviations and notes

LMS—London Missionary Society
PMS—Paris (Evangelical) Missionary Society
Rd(s)—Rixdollar(s)

CA—Cape Town Archives Repository
Auxiliary—*Report of the missions in South Africa, and of the Auxiliaries, in connection with the London Missionary Society* (Cape Town). Annual.
BMB—*Berliner Missionsberichte*. Journal of the Berlin Missionary Society.
CWMA—Council for World Mission Archives (Zug: IDC, 1978). *Microfiche edition of LMS Archives*.
Hodgson—*The journals of the Rev.T.L. Hodgson, 1821–1831*; ed. R.I. Cope (Johannesburg: Witwatersrand University Press, 1977)
Philip—John Philip, *Researches in South Africa* (London: James Duncan, 1828)
Report—*The report of the Directors to the (...) general meeting of the Missionary Society, usually called the London Missionary Society* (London). Annual.
Schreiner—*The missionary letters of Gottlob Schreiner, 1837–1846*; ed. Karel Schoeman (Cape Town: Human & Rousseau, 1991)

One mile equals approximately 1,6 kilometres.
One foot equals approximately 30 centimetres.

1.
Jan Goeyman—James Clark (1822–1827)

As white settlers penetrated deeper into the interior of the Cape Colony during the second half of the eighteenth century, the indigenous inhabitants of the country, the Bushmen, were compelled to fall back before them, and their existence became increasingly threatened. When the London Missionary Society (LMS) began its work in South Africa in 1799, it therefore immediately established a station for these people under J.J. Kicherer at Bly Vooruitzicht on the Sak River, in the present Fraserburg district. The work was subsequently transferred to a neighbouring station known as Zak River, but owing to its unfavourable situation and the frequent absences of the missionary, it never prospered. In practice Zak River soon became a station for the Basters or people of "mixed blood", and was finally abandoned when Kicherer entered the ministry of the Dutch Church in 1806.

After the visit of the Revd John Campbell of the LMS to South Africa in 1813, a new attempt was made to evangelise the Bushmen, which led to the establishment of a number of mission stations, "school places" and "institutions"[1] in the vicinity of the Orange River, beyond the then Northern Frontier of the Colony. What is particularly notable about this development is the promi-

---

1. A "school place" was a mission post formed around a catechist or teacher. An "institution", in mission terms, was an independent community supporting itself by agriculture or other means, under missionary control.

nent role played in it by coloured converts from the existing LMS stations, either as general assistants to the white missionaries or as independent catechists and teachers.

The most important of these new foundations was Toornberg (also called Torenberg, Tooverberg and Genadeberg), established in 1814 under the Dutch missionary Erasmus Smit, assisted by Jan Goeyman, a Baster who had been baptised with his family at Zak River; followed by Hephzibah, founded in 1816 under Goeyman and W.F. Corner, a black missionary from Demerara.[2] In addition, three "school places" or mission outposts were set up further inland, where Khoi teachers were to work under the general supervision of the LMS missionaries at Griquatown. One was at Konnah on the Colonial side of the Orange River, where two men known only as Kruisman and David were living in 1820,[3] while the other two were to the north of the river: Ramah, which came into being in about 1817, under Piet Sabba and Andries Pretorius,[4] and Philippolis, where Jan Goeyman was placed in 1822 by Dominee Abraham Faure of Graaff-Reinet, acting informally as coadjutor to Dr John Philip, the Superintendent of the LMS in South Africa.[5]

In all these cases small groups of coloured Christian families, Basters or Khoikhoi, either accompanied the missionary, teacher or catechist, or else soon gathered around him. Some of them came from the former mission at Zak River and had followed Kicherer to Graaff-Reinet after he had become minister of the Dutch there, participating actively in local mission work, and when the mission for the Bushman was established at Toornberg, permission was given by the Landdrost of Graaff-Reinet for '5 Hottentots with their families to accompany Br. Smit'.[6] Likewise, when James Read travelled to the interior two years later to begin a mission to the Tlhaping at Lattakoo (Dithakong), a number of Khoi families from his congregation at Bethelsdorp came with him to assist in the work.[7] When it was proposed in 1820 that Goeyman should start a mission for the Bushmen at Koningfontein *(the modern Maropeng), beyond Kuruman, permission was requested by Campbell from the Colonial authorities for him to be accompanied by*

three bastard Hottentots who were connected in this very way with our station at Toornberg, (...) to set agoing the proposed mission to the Bushmen at the Koning. (...) If this proposal be agreeable, a few pounds of powder will be absolutely necessary for protection in supporting them by shooting game untill the corn which they may sow shall be gathered in.[8]

So too at Ramah Campbell during his second visit to South Africa in the same year found two Griqua families, with their cattle, as "companions and helpers" to the teachers.[9]

When the zealous young missionary Robert Moffat began work in the Transorange in 1820, first at Griquatown and subsequently at Lattakoo, after the recall of James Read to the Colony in 1820, he overthrew most of what had been done here by the previous generation of missionaries. In the course of his violent reforms, most of the coloured mission assistants were dismissed from the service of the LMS or otherwise alienated, and as they

2. Toornberg was situated on the site of the modern town of Colesberg, and Hephzibah near the modern Petrusville in the Northern Cape.
3. Konnah appears to have been to the east of the modern Hopetown.
4. Ramah has survived as a farm on the boundary line between the Free State and Northern Cape, 3km to north of the Orange River. An article on Pretorius has been published in Schoeman, *The early mission*.
5. Faure, who had been ordained in the Netherlands in 1817, had studied for some years at the LMS College at Gosport in England, hence presumably his special interest in the work of the Society.—For Goeyman, see Schoeman, *The early mission*, pp.177–193.
6. *Hertzog-annale* (1956), p.115.
7. For this development as reflected in the career of Andries Pretorius, see Schoeman, *The early mission*, pp.206–214.
8. CWMA 96 (26.9.1820).
9. *S.A. Historical Journal* 29 (Nov. 1993), 135.

were Christians, they tended also to gather around the scattered mission outposts already existing in the area, which thus developed into small centres of Khoi or Baster settlement.

This second attempt at a Bushman mission was likewise not destined to succeed, partly because the Bushmen themselves still refused to co-operate, partly because the isolated catechists and teachers were not supported adequately by the LMS, and partly because of continued conflicts between the missionaries and white farmers in the vicinity. By 1818 both Toornberg and Hephzibah had been closed down on the orders of the Government as a result of friction with white incomers, and because of insufficient supervision the work at the school places failed to develop. Konnah and Ramah are mentioned for the last time in 1824,[10] and eventually only Philippolis was to survive and prosper, though ultimately not as a station for the Bushmen.

The first known mention of Philippolis occurs in the journal of the Wesleyan missionary T.L. Hodgson, who visited it in November 1822 on his way into the interior and stated that "This institution was commenced about 6 months ago", thus dating its foundation to the autumn of that year.[11]

At present there is [sic] but twenty Bushmen, including children, at the institution, though the usual number of residents is about 60, the remainder having gone to a distance in search of what they term rice, the eggs of the ants, which they procure as food from the large anthills seen upon the road. The Native teacher here is considered a good man and in his manners there is a modesty very prepossessing. He lives in [a] reed house (or hartebeast), but is building one of bricks dried in the sun, as well as a school,[12] both [of] which are suitable for the place.[13]

The first official appearance of the station in the annual report of the LMS published early in 1824 was not encouraging, however.

An attempt has been lately made at Philippolis (a place so called from respect to the Rev. Dr Philip) to revive the mission to the Boscheman, under the Hottentot[14] teacher Jan Goeyman, who was sent there for this purpose. We are sorry to say that no discernible success has as yet attended his labours. He complains that he cannot acquire the requisite influence over the people, and thinks a European missionary would succeed where he has failed.[15]

The Bushmen were a nomadic race and never inclined to settle permanently, much to the chagrin of the missionaries who tried to evangelise them. While this may largely explain Goeyman's lack of success, in a letter to the Landdrost of Graaff-Reinet, Andries Stockenstrom, early in 1825, however, he complained specifically of the unruliness of the people under him ("de volk die onder mij behoor"), by which he meant the Khoi or Baster families who had gathered around him in the manner described above. This group of early settlers was to remain a sizeable portion of the population of Philippolis, and to be a source of unrest on the station for many years. A potentially more serious threat to Goeyman's work, however, was the presence in the vicinity of malcontents from Griquatown who had settled in the mountainous region south of the modern Lückhoff, acquiring the name "Bergenaars" and carrying out cattle raids over a very wide area.

10. The work at Ramah was to be revived in 1844, under supervision of the missionary at Philippolis.
11. Hodgson, p.69.
12. Originally "church" in the manuscript. In the earlier stages of a mission the same building was often used for both purposes.
13. Source: Hodgson, p.68.
14. Here as elsewhere it should be noted that the term "Hottentot" was at this time used to refer to Khoikhoi, Griquas and Basters indiscriminately.
15. Source: Report (1824), p.113.

On these recurrent problems, Goeyman expressed himself as follows to Stockenstrom some three years after he had begun working at Philippolis.[16]

Philippolis, den 15 Januarij [1825]

Myn heer, met dese gelegendheid kan ik niet na laat om u te melde hoe het hier gaat. Ik had rede om dankbaar te wees, vandat myn heer hier is geweest,[17] is het nu tog so ver met de Grikwas dat sy de vremde natsi ongehinderd laat,[18] in [*=en*] ook is hier by my sommege van haar na die tyd voor de eerste maal in de Gods diens gewees, bijsonders Andries Hendriks scheijn goeij voornemens te hebben.[19] Maar de volk die onder mij behoor, blyf ongehoorsaam in [*=en*] gaat gedurig sonder een pas binne de Kolonie, de tolk van mijn heef twee ossen verhandel sonder dat hij een pas van mij heef. Sulke *ongehoorsaam* [word or part of word illegible] volk had ik, als het haar wort toe gelaat, dan sal de Grikwas seker daar de voet op neem, dan raak als weer in waenorder, daarom is myn ootmoedige versoek aan mijn heer dat sulks mag verhindert wort als mijn heer belief. De os die de Konstabels gestool heef, die heef sij weer afgegeven.

Ik blijf u dienswellege dienaar, Johannes Jacobus Goeijman.[20]

Among the Macmillan Papers at Rhodes House, Oxford, there is a note by a modern researcher summarising a letter by Goeyman of the same date and with similar contents, apparently addressed to Dr Philip in Cape Town.[21] *The note includes the sentence: "Complains of attacks by Griquas, particularly of thefts by the constables, Kleine Adam, Old Johannes, Andries Pretorius, Cupidos David Jan etc." (punctuation and capitalization as in the original). "Constables" in this case would appear not to indicate local officials, but members of the Constabel or Konstabel family mentioned in Goeyman's letter.*

In August 1825 Dr Philip himself visited the station in a

course of an extensive journey into the interior, and gave an unenthusiastic account of what he found there in his Researches in South Africa, *which were published shortly afterwards.*

The site of this mission is about five hours' journey with a waggon from the ford;[22] but there is not a sufficiency of water to irrigate enough of land to enable a large body of people to support themselves by gardening and agriculture. We found several Bushmen belonging to the station receiving instructions; but the pleasure we experienced on visiting it arose more from the hope of what might be done than from any thing which had as yet been effected. Mr Clark, a European, who had accompanied me from the Colony, has now the superintendence of this mission, and by the blessing of God upon his labours I hope soon to hear of its prosperity.[23]

The Annual Report of the LMS published the following year was similarly vague on the subject of the changes introduced by Philip at Philippolis.

When Dr Philip in the course of his late tour arrived here, he found Goeyman devoting himself chiefly to agricultural pursuits,

16. In transcribing Goeyman's letter, some punctuation has been introduced, but it has further been left unaltered. Both his handwriting and command of Dutch are notably better than those of the majority of the white fieldcornets whose correspondence has been preserved in the same official files.
17. A reference to Stockenstrom's visit to the area in October 1824.
18. The reference is presumably to Sotho-Tswana refugees preyed upon by the Griqua banditti.
19. Andries Hendriks, an emigrant from Griquatown, was a prominent Bergenaar, and an uncle of the later Secretary to the Griqua Raad or Council of Philippolis, Hendrik Hendrickze.
20. Source: CA, reference not noted.
21. Rhodes House, Oxford, MSS.Afr.s.316, p.413.
22. The route from the former Toornberg through the Orange River.
23. Source: Philip II, 90.

and, of course, not paying the requisite attention to the object of his mission. Upon Dr Philip prescribing a different plan of proceeding, the teacher, not choosing to conform to it, sent in his resignation. Mr James Clark, formerly a member of Dr Philip's church at Cape Town, has been stationed at Philippolis in the room of Goeyman.[24]

> Reports appearing in the mission publications were, however, not only drastically edited (many of the missionaries were uneducated men and unable to express themselves with the requisite elegance), but on occasion also heavily censored. As far as Goeyman was concerned, Philip had in fact during his stay at Philippolis investigated charges of adultery brought against the teacher by Andries Constabel, as a result of which he stated, "I consider it my duty as the agent of the L.M. Society to suspend Jan Goeyman from the performance of any religious duties."[25]
>
> John Clark, who was now put in charge of the mission, was a Scot, about 36 years of age and unmarried, who is known to have been working previously as brickmaker on the LMS mission station at Hankey in the Eastern Province, and Philip had probably intended to place him on one of the stations in the interior as an artisan. Judging by his letters, he was not an educated man, though his knowledge of Dutch appears to have been fluent, if faulty, and he hardly seems to have been prepared for his new responsibilities, to which was added the violent resentment of Goeyman at being supplanted. A confrontation between the two men soon took place, which is recorded in the testimony of Andries Stoffels as taken down by Clark: the latter's attempt to record Stoffels' colloquial Afrikaans in his own rendering of Dutch produced an extremely vivid document which deserves to be quoted in its original form.[26]

Philipolis, Thursday, 29th Sepr. 1825

Getuige, dat Jan Goeyman had Mynheer Clark geroep van de straat af met een groote stem, toen dat Mynheer Clark was by myn op het Bushmen pampion [=*pompoen*] land om water daarop te lei, end dat Mynheer Clark had geantwoord dat hy Jan Goeyman kan liever by hem kome op de land, ende dat Jan Goeyman end Mynheer Clark had gegaan tesaam tot Mynheer Clarks woon kammer in het kerk, maar dat Jan Goeyman in quadheid had de kerk durhingsel gebrik [=*gebreek*], ende omdat Jan Goeyman had zyn wrouwe [=*vrouw*] gebring, alsoo had Mynheer Clark myn geroep end Meetje Witboy, Katrena De Bruyn end Anna Davids als getuigen. End toen had Jan Goeyman tot Mynheer Clark geseg dat hy, Doctor Philip end Mynheer Bartlet had tesaamen gespaan om hem, Jan Goeyman, te onderdruck,[27] en dat Doctor Philip had hem onrecht gedaan, ende dat hy, Jan Goeyman, sal niet onderdanig [zyn] tot Mynheer Clark of tot Doctor Philips order als sulks,[28] maar tot Mynheer Faure[s] order dat hy, Jan Goeyman, by hem heeft, dat deze Philipolis was aangerecht by Mynheer Faure.[29] Ende Jan Goeyman had gezeg voor ons dat het is door de Sendeling dat de Bergenaars had de Caffres beesten ont-

24. Source: Report (1826), p.82.
25. CWMA 125 ("Minutes of an investigation...", 11.8.1825).
26. Some elucidation of the obscure Dutch has been given in the footnotes, in the form of extracts from Clark's own translation of this document, which accompanied it, but for an independent account in English of what happened, see the letter by Clark which follows.
27. John Bartlett was an Englishman who in 1811, while employed as a blacksmith in Cape Town, had offered his services to the LMS as a missionary, and now accompanied Philip on his journey to the interior, where he was placed in charge of the mission at Campbell. He was married to one of Goeyman's sisters,
28. "to Doctor Philip['s] order to recognize Mr Clark as head of this Institution".
29. "it was Mr Faure that established the place".

nomen.³⁰ Maar toen had Mynheer Clark geantwoord dat hy, Mynheer Clark, weet daarvan niets, maar dat hy, Mynheer Clark, moet gehoorzame wees tot de Genootschaap[s] orders door Doctor Philip, end dat hy denk so moet Jan Goeyman ook. Maar Jan Goeyman had gezeg hy wil niet onder Mynheer Clark staan so als Doctor Philip heeft hem hier gesteld, end dat had hy, Jan Goeyman, geweet, hy sou noitni toegelaat Mynheer Clark of zyn goederen in de kerk te komen, end dat hy zou zyn goederen buite trek end stu[k]ken[d] smyt, end dat als Mynheer Clark of iemand sal zyn ploeg neme sonder hem te vraag, hy sal hem slaan op de oor. Ende Jan Goeyman had gevloek voor ons alle op de straat,³¹ viz. voor Meetje Whitboy, Anna Davids, Katrena De Bruyn, myn ende oock Jefrouw Goeyman end Mynheer Clark, end daar was van de school kinderen daarby. End Jan Goeyman had gezeg dat Mynheer Clark had gehoor dat Jan Goeyman had gezaag [=*gezaaid*] op een buitenfontein van de Hottentots,³² maar Mynheer Clark geantwoord dat hy had gehoor dat Jan Goeyman had geploeg by de rivier van het Boor voor hy had op Philipolis gekome met Doctor Philip,³³ ende oock dat Mynheer Clark weet dat Jan Goeyman heeft gezaag op Bushman fontien.³⁴ Ende verder had Jan Goeyman gezeg tot Mynheer Clark dat hy nu ryde sal tot Graaff Reinet,³⁵ end als Mynheer Clark wil hy sal zyn briefe neme met hem. End wy verder getuige dat Mynheer Clark had altoos ordentelyk gesproken tot Jan Goeyman en zyn wrouwe, endat dat Meetje Whitboy, Katrine De Bruyn, Anna Davids, myself, Jefrouw Goeyman en Mynheer Clark waar alles dat tegenwoordig was van de grootvolk.³⁶ Ende dat Jefrouw Goeyman was quad tegen Mynheer Clark oock oer de selvde order,³⁷ maar Mynheer Clark antwoord dat hy had niets met Jefrouw Goeyman te doen in die saak.

Getuigen van de boven[staande] is, van die tyd af dat Mynheer Clark had ons geroep: Andries Stoffels, zyn + merk; Anna Davids, haar + merk; Meitje Wetbooy.³⁸

This declaration was sent to Philip by Clark with an English translation and the following covering note:

Explanation of the above

Understanding that Jan Goeyman had sown no corn for the Bushmen this season, I sent for (what I was informed was) the Society plough, Jan being not at home, and ploughed here a piece of land for pompens [=*pumpkins*] for the Bushmen (a necessary work), and on Jan Goeyman's coming home,[39] I understood from him that owing to the weakness of the fountain there would not be water enough for his corn here (that he has sown for himself) and all the people's gardens too, and that therefore, since the corn was sown, that the people plant but little in their gardens this year, to which I consented and spoke to the people, and consequently I planted less pompens here than I would have otherwise done; but on the 29th September, seeing Jan's Caffre digging a piece of ground in his garden, I went to Jan there and asked him if he meant to plant. He answered, Yes. I mentioned that he had better not plant much more here, as there were yet several of the people not returned from following Dr P. [*to Griquatown*] who would want water for their gardens also, and

30. The Sotho-Tswana refugees on or around the station.
31. "and further that Jan Goeyman hereby did curse, saying damn him".
32. "that it was from the Hottentots that he, Mr Clark, heard that he, Jan Goeyman, had sown corn lately by [an]other fountain for himself".
33. "that he [Clark] had heard from the Boors first before he came here".
34. Boesmansfontein, a farm near Philippolis belonging to the LMS.
35. i.e., to Dominee Faure.
36. "Adults".
37. "And that Mrs Goeyman conducted herself unsuitably against Mr Clark on the above occasion."
38. "I have also Katrina De Bruyn's signature by me in substance to the above, James Clark."—Source of quotation: CWMA 125.
39. He had apparently accompanied Philip to Griquatown.

that I would not [=*nor?*] can promise him water for his corn and a large garden besides, to which he answered, the people had their corn land by other fountains, but not he. I answered that I am informed he has also corn growing by other fountains, and I mentioned where, but I told him that I only meant to inform him that I could not promise him water for his corn land here and a large garden whilst other people's gardens suffered, He asked me if he was head of this Institution. I answered that Dr Philip had placed me as head here. He said he was head, and that he would not recognize me as head. I mentioned that I could shew him otherwise, and I came away from him. He followed me very angry out of his garden, but I went to water the pompen land. He then called me (as above mentioned) from the street with a loud, angry tone, to which I answered rather to come near me and speak to me. He came, saying he wished me to shew him that Dr P. had placed me as head of this Institution, and in consequence of his noisy manner I went with him as above, but seeing him bringing his wife, Mrs Goeyman, and breaking the hinges of the door of the house wherein I lodge, I called the above individuals as witnesses, when the above conversation and circumstances occurred.

I am sorry to say that Jan Goeyman conducted himself so and cursed before the people and espicialy the children that came around, and were it not for his mistakeing views, his unchristian disposition and conduct on that occasion, and thus his bad example as a missionary, which may spread in the world, and espicialy as he is considered connected with the London Missionary Society, I would not have considered myself bound to have informed you of the above unhappy occurrance. Having done so, I leave it to you and to others to judge what should be done. You have already his own hand writing that he is of no use here.[40] I might also mentioned that Mrs Goeyman conducted herself unsuitably against me on that occassion also.

I remain your obedient, humble servant, James Clark

Philipolis, 4th Octr. 1825
Jan rode from this [place] that day.[41]

Finding on arrival at Graaff-Reinet that Dominee Faure had recently removed to Cape Town, Goeyman sent him a letter of complaint, to which, however, he received no satisfaction, Faure informing him that he had been appointed "as an assistant only, and not as a principal",[42] and that he was now dismissed. He therefore removed from Philippolis, but remained in the district, where he was still mentioned as an itinerating schoolteacher as late as 1834.

40. Goeyman seems to have written to Philip himself.
41. Source: CWMA 125.
42. CWMA 125.(6.11.1825).

2.
The Griquas at Philippolis (1826)

During his journey into the interior in 1825, Dr Philip had conceived an ambitious plan for the LMS stations there which was to affect the future development of Philippolis profoundly. According to this the armed and mounted Griquas living in the vicinity of the Orange River were to form a bulwark along the Northern Frontier of the Cape Colony, preventing further encroachment by white farmers on the one hand, while on the other protecting the Colonists against attacks by Mzilikazi and his amaNdebele then living beyond the Vaal. The guiding and controlling role in this scheme was to be played by the LMS missionaries stationed here, and early in 1826 the mission assistant Peter Wright, in whom Philip had great confidence, was ordained as a missionary and placed at Griquatown.

After the missionary protegé Andries Waterboer had been elected Kaptyn at Griquatown in 1820, the former Kaptyn, Adam Kok II, had left the area, and at the time of Philip's visit to the interior he was living on the Riet River with a motley group of followers. Interfering vigorously in local affairs, Philip urged this group to elect Kok formally as their leader and persuaded the Bergenaar raiders to accept his authority. Kok's election having been duly recognised by the British authorities at the Cape, Wright now gave him and his people permission to settle in the Philippolis region, where a third Griqua Captaincy thus came into being alongside those already existing at Griquatown and Campbell. Shortly afterwards, Kok established himself at the *mission station, which thus became his capital.*

James Clark gave the following account of these developments in a letter written in September 1827, which appears to have been addressed to Andries Stockenstrom at Graaff-Reinet. The "Hottentot inhabitants of Philippolis" referred to were the Khoi and Basters who had settled there around Goeyman on the establishment of the station.

Immediately on Dr Philip leaving this country for England,[1] the Hottentot inhabitants of Philippolis began to build for themselves a considerable number of good houses and *other works*, both on that station and the neighbouring fountains around. They also began to cultivate a considerable quantity of corn. But several months afterward (now 16 months ago) Mr Wright, missionary at Griquatown, arrived at Philippolis on his way to the Bergenaars then lying at the Moder River,[2] and informed me that he was appointed their missionary, that Dr Philip had requested that he might endevour to bring *them back to Griquatown*, but that in the event of their refusal, he was at liberty to form a station among them where they choosed, even at Philippolis, and in that case I am my people must commence a station for Bushmen at the Caledon River.

Mr Wright proceeded to the Bergenaars and gave them Dr Philip's authority to occupy Philippolis, which they consented to do. Soon after this an outpost near Philippolis was attacked by a party of Caffres, which threatened very soon to return, and not doubting Mr Wright's authority, we called in the Bergenaars to

1. On his return from the interior, Philip left immediately for England, where he was to spend four years.
2. This was presumably when Wright was on his way from the Eastern Province to his new station at Griquatown. The reference is presumably to Kok and his immediate followers on the Lower Riet River (then often called the Modder) and to the Bergenaar dissidents from Griquatown.

Philippolis, and I even gave them the station over *in writting*, [3] in order that they might be inclined to protect it. The Bergenaars were not, however, inclined to protect it, but left it and went towards the Griqua Country (where, by the by, as above mentioned, Dr Philip originally wished them to go),[4] and they requested Adam Kok, their *Kaptein*, to accompany them, which he refused to do.[5]

The attack "by a party of Caffres" which precipitated the arrival of Kok and his people at Philippolis is not particularly well documented. It seems to have occurred in May 1826, and it is mentioned in a lengthy report on South African mission affairs to the Directors of the LMS compiled some months after the event by Richard Miles, acting Superintendent of the Society during Philip's absence in England.

The statement which I sent of an attack by the Caffres upon an outstation of Philippolis has proved, as I had too much reason to fear, correct. Mr Clark states in his account of this melancholy affair:

"At about eleven o'clock at night (Sabbath night) I was awoke out of sleep by Hans the Bushman in a great hurry, saying that a party of Caffres had just attacked Bushman Fontein farm and had murdered old Adam Krotz, his wife and daughter, and several other women and their children, in number more than 26 persons, who were within were burned to death in their houses or assegaied in attempting to flee out of them, and that the Caffres had also taken away all the cattle. I requested our people would seek their horses and attempt to rescue the cattle. At daybreak nine of our Hottentots set off and followed the track of the Caffres, and found them in the afternoon, just having entered a deep kloof or cave with all the cattle. By our people repeatedly firing into it, the cattle at length spring [*sic*] out, and were all rescued again.

"In the meantime, early in the morning, I rode out with a

number of our women, and buried the dead. We prayed and buried, but were obliged to leave the horrid sight so quickly as possible. The various positions of the dead was [*sic*] most distressing to behold. I brought away three who were still living, and one had got to Philippolis before me. Thirty-one persons have in the whole perished by this catastrophe."

In consequence of this dreadful affair, Mr Clark sent to Griquatown [*sic*] to Dam Kok for assistance and protection, and it appears to be his intention to remain there. Mr Clark expresses his fears that he shall be obliged to remove to some other place, as the Bushmen are averse to living amongst the Griquas.[6]

Miles's earlier "statement" referred to was a letter dated 17 July 1826, with which he had enclosed an unidentified newspaper clipping quoting a "letter from the Frontier, June 29th" which described "a most shocking occurrence" which had taken place "a few weeks ago"; according to Miles this letter had been written by "Mr Robertson of Graaff Reinet".[7] "Bushman Fontein farm" where the massacre took place was Boesmansfontein, 10 km to the north-west of Philippolis, of which the newspaper report stated: "this farm belonged more particularly to the missionary, being kept for his use, and for the support of the Bushmen who attended the Institution". The same report described the attackers as "a number of Caffers who had formed themselves into a body, and had been in the habit of committing depredations on their neighbours". The term "Caffers", in various spellings, at this time usually referred to the amaXhosa, of whom there were a

---

3. Note added in the original: "[*word illegible*] this is the document they attempted to show you lately".
4. The Bergenaar element among the followers of Adam Kok II soon left him to return to the Griquatown Captaincy.
5. Source: CA, 1/GR 10/6 Clark—Stockenstrom (10.9.1827).
6. Source: CWMA 134 (16.1.1827).
7. CWMA 131.

number living in scattered groups in the vicinity of the Orange River. Andrew Smith, visiting the Philippolis area late in 1834, stated, however, that the murders at Boesmansfontein had been committed by "Basutu" in search of cattle stolen by the Bergenaars which they believed to have tracked to the farm,[8] and it seems likely that they were in fact Sotho or Tswana refugees.[9]

Given Clark's unprotected situation, his panic in these circumstances was understandable, and the most obvious course was indeed to call in the help of Adam Kok and his armed and mounted followers. In practice, however, the coming of the Griquas to Philippolis meant the further dispersal of the Bushmen in the area and the effective end of any mission work for them that might still have been undertaken on the station. A second problem was the conflict which very soon arose between the Griqua incomers and the Khoikhoi or Basters already living there, and loath to recognise the authority of the Griqua Kaptyn and Raad, this well-defined group of church members and mission supporters—the "Old Inhabitants" as they soon came to be called—appealed for help to their former missionary James Read, who had meanwhile resumed work at Bethelsdorp. Tension between the Old Inhabitants and the Griquas was to continue for many years, involving and ultimately bringing to grief almost all the missionaries stationed at Philippolis

Within a year of the Griquas' arrival, James Clark himself had come to find the situation untenable, and he expressed his views to Peter Wright at Griquatown in a letter dated 10 April 1827. Clark's letter has not been traced, but a good deal of information on these developments at Philippolis may be obtained from Wright's reply on 10 May, in which he reacted sharply and at some length to his colleague's implicit criticism of the role he himself had played in the events.[10]

(…) Philippolis is now worthy [of] the name of a public or missionary institution. Previous to the additions that have been made,[11] its name as a missionary station was really, my Brother, like a mere trick played upon the religious public. The state in which I found things fourteen [?] months ago at Philippolis[12] certainly agreed with your representations sent to Dr Philip previous to my leaving Cape Town, and justified the proposal *you* then made of removing the Bushman Station and *your* recommendation that *Adam Kok and his people* should remove to Philippolis.

With respect to Dr Philip's being justified in acceding to the above proposal in the event of my finding things as you represented them, [this?] is clear to any person of a public spirit. When you remember that *nothing of a missionary nature was [illegible] doing nor had been done* from the commencement of the station, with the exception of the erection of a number of small mud houses by a few persons who wish to be considered as assistants in the mission work, and for this very reason, of course, the least (or rather, not at all) intitled to the privilege of monopolising a number of fountains in a large territory which ought to be applied to a public use.[13] You know the station went in the name of a Bushman station, but you remember you were not able to produce me any direct effects of the labour of missionaries amongst the Bushmen under the means of grace at the station. I

8. Smith:Diary I, 185.
9. Large numbers of Batswana and Basotho had fled the devastation caused on the Highveld by the invasions and forced migrations of the Difaqane earlier in the decade, and the subsequent depredations of Kora, Bergenaar and other raiders.
10. This letter has been filed in the LMS archives under 1826, and dated "10 May 1826" in the typed list of Incoming Letters. As far as the microfiche version can be deciphered, however, it seems to be dated "10 May 1827", which would moreover correspond to the sequence of events described by Wright. The earlier dating does not seem feasible.
11. The establishment of the Griquas here.
12. This is not clear on the microfiche, but "fourteen months" would agree with a visit by Wright to Philippolis in March 1826 while on his way to Griquatown.
13. A reference to Old Inhabitants.

found also that when I visited the station you frequently declared to me that the station could not become a Bushman station, and urged the necessity of commencing in another quarter in order to succeed.

One chief reason you gave me for the above declarations was that no Bushmen would ever [*settle at the mission?*][14] as long as the Griquas were in the neighbourhood, and particularly *so long as there were any Oorlams*[15] *(Old Inhabitants) residing at the station*, who had been detected in using secret means to prejudice the minds of the Bushmen and frighten them away, and even some of those who had previously been engaged in the Bushmen mission were strongly suspected of being the principal persons in this shameful conduct. I allude now to Pretoris, of whose bad character you heard from Dr Philip himself.[16] At the time he expressed a wish that Pretoris should be removed from the country.

This state of things at Philippolis, together with finding such a immense population connected with A. Kok of upwards of 300 families of Griquas, Coranna and Bechuannas on the banks of the Modder [=*Riet*] River without any abiding place, destitute of the Gospel, desiring the means of grace and pleading to go to Philippolis, induced me to make the communication to them that they had Dr Philip's authority to proceed to that station.

Now, my dear Brother, notwithstanding this business being finally settled, and which (by the bye) originated with yourself, yet you urge me for advice in the affair. You say Pretoris has been to Bethelsdorp and complained to the missionaries, who say that Dr Philip had no right to allow the Griquas to remove to Philippolis and that they [*2 lines illegible*] you have entirely changed your sentiments in the affair on the ground of such unfounded stories of such a character as that of Pretoris, and that A. Kok has allowed him to create such unpleasantness and met with such violence. Were the stories which he brought from Bethelsdorp facts, you need not be told that they are of no authority, any more than if they had come from the missionaries of the East and West Indies.

I cannot think that you can have forgotten the character you gave me of Pretoris' family, how that he was an active agent of the Bergenaars during the time of their impoverishing the Caffres[17] and distroying them in such great numbers, that he was at that time Rds1600 indebted to the Farmers in the neighbourhood for horses and contraband articles,[18] which he had purchased for the marauders to enable them to execute their cruel expeditions against the poor Caffres, that his premises had been a regular rendezvous for them, that the great number of cattle he then possessed, which I judged at the time I saw them consisted of several hundreds, were the cattle which he had received from the Bergenaars as payment for the abovementioned articles, that he refused to pay the Boors his debts, and dared not set his foot over the River for fear of being seized. You also stated to me that his moral conduct on the place was bad and his influence pernicious as it respects the Sabbath, for which from his conduct he appears to have no regard; that in the presence of a respectable English gentleman (Dr Gill),[19] in the very face of your own re-

14. The words between brackets are illegible on the microfiche here transcribed.
15. Just as the term "Hottentots" was used loosely to refer to Khoikhoi, Griquas and Basters, "Oorlams" was used vaguely to indicate westernised "Hottentots".
16. Probably Andries Pretorius Sr, a convert from Bethelsdorp, who had accompanied the missionary James Read into the interior in 1815, but had since become alienated from the mission. At the time of his conversion he had proudly referred to himself as a "Bushman". His son of the same name is mentioned by Wright later in the same letter and clearly distinguished as "Junr".
17. Here again the Tswana and Sotho refugees in the Orange River area are probably meant in general, rather than the amaXhosa.
18. The reference is to white farmers.
19. Probably Dr William Gill, of Malmesbury in the Cape Colony and later Somerset East, who is known to have paid several visits to the interior during the 1820s.

monstrance and actually at the time your people were going to church, he persisted in digging out the foundation of his house on the Sabbath day. And you also remember bringing me to the Caffres who had been sold to a merchant by A. Pretoris (Junr.) for gunpowder.

Now although this fellow Pretoris was employed at Philippolis by the Society, yet, being the character above described, the Society can no longer acknowledge him in any way, and being on this side of the River, without any written authority from the Colonial Government, we, my Brother, as missionaries dare not in any way countenance him.

Now, my dear Brother, I feel intirely at a loss to give you any advice in the affair in question, owing to the very unsteady and strange line of conduct you are pursuing, and the opposite sentiments which you discover in your last letters upon the subject.

Your letters to me from time to time reporting the circumstances of the station are now all before me, together with a document you gave A. Kok on his arrival at the station, and as you appear to keep no copies of your letters, and intirely forget what you write, I would just remind you of the most important of the particulars you have written me applying to the circumstances of the station.

In a letter to me on my way from Philippolis to this dated May 29 [1826], informing me of the awful catastrophe which occurred at Bushman Fountain, you add, "that it is impossible for you and your people to remain at the station any longer, that your people were removing to the Colony, and that you were coming to the neighbourhood of Griqua Town, and that you had already sent for A. Kok to the station." From another letter, dated 18 July, I find you inform me that "A. Kok had according to your request come with all his people to Philippolis during your absence at Graaf Reinet, and that you left home in perfect confidence that he would come while you were away". You further informed me by the same letter, "that you found it absolutely necessary to remain at Philippolis, at least for a time, otherwise Dam and all his people would leave it, and in the event of that, the station would be completely abandoned, as your people would not at all be able to withstand an attack from the Caffres".

From the document put into my hands which you gave to A. Kok dated 22 July 1826, consisting of four separate strange articles, I find you have not only ceded the *station* to all intents and purposes to the Captain and his people, which is an act neither you nor the Missionary Society had power to do, but you ceded the *missionary also*, whoever he may be, for ever, so that by your paper he is become to all intents and purposes a subject of the Captain of Philippolis.

From another letter, dated 21 September last, you inform me of the renewed attack of the Caffres on your neighbourhood amongst the Farmers, and that in consequence A. Kok would leave the station should you remove. You further state in this letter, as it respects the Old Inhabitants, in the event of their remaining at Philippolis, and [being] allowed to cultivate their outside fountains,[20] that "nothing of a missionary nature would be effected amongst them, as from their various occupations at their farms, such as watering cornland, keeping off the birds, cutting it down, planting tobacco, &c., &c., they were generally absent from the village, and that those who had no corn, but depended upon their milk, say they cannot long graze at Philippolis and they must go with their cattle, [and] that this is the case at present".

You find from the above extracts from your own letters not only that nothing was in doing, or could be done, of a missionary description, *according to the old system,* but that had it not been for the presence of A. Kok and his people to protect the station, it would long since have been abandoned, and further, according

---

20. i.e., outlying fountains, at a distance from the settlement.

to your own declaration, that if you had found any proper reasons why he should not be allowed to remain at the place, you could have adopted a very easy method of getting him away.[21]

Early in 1827 John Melvill, the former Government Agent at Griquatown, was placed at Philippolis at Clark's request to assist him in the work, the intention being that Clark should remain free to devote himself to the Bushmen. Writing to to the Directors of the LMS in London on 8 June of that year, Melvill enclosed a copy of Wrigh's letter to Clark quoted above, and gave his own comments on the situation.

I am happy to say that I succeeded in gaining the affections of the people,[22] and Brother Clark giving it out that he was destined for the Bushmen, they applied to me to remain as their missionary. The state of things was becoming more encouraging, there were 100 children in the school and the congregations more than the place of worship could [*illegible*] hold; but unhappily a difference took place between the Old Inhabitants and the Griquas, which has caused some confusion, and very much discouraged the Chief A. Kok and cooled his zeal to promote the good cause. The disturbance originated in the visit of A. Pretoris to Bethelsdorp, who reported on his return that you had no right to give the station to the Griquas, and that the missionaries sent "orders" to all the Old Inhabitants that they should no longer submit to the authority of A. Kok, but that they must remain as Society's people,[23] &c., &c. I cannot enter into all the particulars of this unpleasant affair. It is sufficient to say that Dam's [=*Adam Kok*] feelings were much hurt that missionaries should interfere in such matters, tho' it is to be hoped that the missionaries sent no such order.

Mr Clark, who was requested by the Old Inhabitants to be their "Captain", very properly (as he had himself recommended that they should submit to the Chief while they remained in the country[24]) declined such an office, but some [*illegible*] or other he afterwards altered his sentiments and fell in with the alleged [*illegible*] of the missionaries of Bethelsdorp, and [now] sides with the Pretoris party. Being junior missionary, I took no part in the affair, except giving my advice to Br. Clark, and pointing out the danger and inconsistency of his conduct.[25] But he having at length, after losing the confidence of the Griquas, resigned the superintendence of the mission to me, it became my duty to endeavour to settle the business. I found it necessary to get the advice of Mr Wright, and to know from him upon what conditions the station was given over. He wrote a letter to Br. Clark (a copy of which I have enclosed),[26] and another to the Chief, who had solicited his influence.

I returned from Griqua Town about a fortnight ago. Just before I went away, Br. Clark seemed to see his error and confessed he had committed himself, and said he would go out to look for a suitable place for a Bushman station, but on my return I found he had been brought about again by the Pretoris party, for he was actually proceeding towards the Caledon River[27] when the [*sic*] Pretoris rode after him and induced him to go to Graaf Reinet, for what purpose I know not, but report says he intends [?] to make this [=*Philippolis*] the Bushman station, and all the Old Inhabitants are said to be coming in from their farms to reside here. He returned from Graaf Reinet four days ago, and set off again the next morning, followed by most of the Old

21. Source: CWMA 130 ("Copy of a letter from Mr Wright to Mr Clark", 16.5.1826).
22. i.e., the Old Inhabitants and Griquas.
23. That is, under the authority of the LMS rather than the Griqua Kaptyn.
24. i.e. the Griqua country (the Philippolis district).
25. " also gave my opinion on the subject to some of the most sensible of the Old Inhabitants, one of whom is decidedly on the side of the Chief, and takes no part in the affair" (note in the margin of the original).
26. Already quoted; see p.26–32 above.
27. Where he intended looking for a suitable site for a station.

Inhabitants, in a NW direction, with an intention, it is said, to collect the Bushmen and bring them here, and just before he set out he told Dam that all the Old Inhabitants were under him.[28]

In this move to establish a new station for himself Clark was able to enlist the support of Andries Stockenstrom, an official remarkably well disposed towards the Bushmen, and there are several letters of Clark to Stockenstrom in which he forcefully argued not only their case, but also that of the Old Inhabitants, with whom he had aligned himself against the Griqua incomers.

"*Now, Sir,*" *Clark declared in a letter dated 10 September 1827, in which he described Philip's original decision to settle the Griquas at Philippolis,*[29]

you will see from the above statement that whatever power Dr Philip may have given Mr Wright in this case, yet for the honour of Dr Philip, he did not not mean to deprive a poor people just emerging out of heathenism of their houses which they were encouraged by their missionary to build in the prospect of enjoying them. The greater part of these works were done after Dr Philip leaving the country consequently could know nothing about them. And I must further add in behalf of Dr Philip that his allowing the Bergenaars to occupy any part of the Bushman Country was in consequence of an extreme case, viz., to lead these people off from their marauding practises and bring them to a settled state of life. Their leaving Philippolis, however, did not answer the end intended,[30] and it surely cannot be argued that because their Kaptain, Adam Kok, and a few of his relatives remained, that he can still claim dominion and posession of the Bushman Country and fill it with Korrannas, Caffres and other Griquas, to the prejudice of the poor Bushmen and of the original inhabitants of Philippolis, placing the former out of the protection of the Colony, and depriving the latter of their property unless they became Griquas, which is neather their interest nor in their power to be, they being inhabitants of the Colony. The fact is, they came over the boundary as assistants to a Bushman station, and they will rather return to it than be incorporated and live under a Griqua Kaptain.[31]

With the sympathetic support of Stockenstrom, Clark was able to obtain the authorisation of the Lieutenant-Governor of the Eastern Province, Sir Richard Bourke, for the removal of the Bushman mission at Philippolis to another site, and in May 1828 he and an assistant, G.A. Kolbe, commenced work on a new station near the confluence of the Orange and the Caledon which was to be known simply as the Bushman Station or the Caledon Institution (now Bethulie). Philippolis was left to James Melvill, the Old Inhabitants and the Griquas.

28. i.e., Clark.—Source of quotation: CWMA 136.
29. This passage is quoted on pp.23–24 above.
30. As mentioned already (p.25 n4 above), a large section of Bergenaars broke away from Kok soon after settling at Philippolis, and resumed their raiding life.
31. Source: CA, 1/GR 10/6.

3.
John Melvill (1827–1831)

In 1822 John Melvill had for idealistic reasons resigned his lucrative post as Government Land Surveyor in Cape Town in order to become Government Agent at Griquatown. In this capacity he seems to have had difficulties with the Kaptyn, Andries Waterboer, and this probably prompted hom to offer his services to the LMS as a missionary in 1826.[1] *While waiting to be accepted by the Directors, he received "a pressing invitation from Mr Clark to come to his assistance" at Philippolis,*[2] *the intention being that he should minister more particularly to the Baster and Griqua section of the population; and he arrived at this station with his family on 10 January 1827. He was 39 years of age, and he and his Cape-born wife, Anna Frederica Stadler, already had eight children, the youngest of whom was not yet six months old; six further children were to be born to them.*

Melvill corresponded directly with the LMS in London, rather than with Wright at Griquatown as did Clark, with the result that his letters from Philippolis have been preserved in the Society's archives. Although they are not distinguished by any great ease of expression, they do at least provide a clearer picture of the station itself and the work done there than was available before.

Melvill's first letter from Philippolis was dispatched in April 1827, and took the form of a journal, the introductory entry in which reads as follows.

The following is the present state of the mission. (...) The people called here the Old Inhabitants are five or six families of Colonial Hottentots who belonged to the Bushman mission, and eight or nine families from the Colony who were allowed to settle here while Jan Goeyman had the management of the station. Some of these came from Bethelsdorp; only part of these persons have regular passes to come beyond the boundary of the Colony.³ Some of these people were formerly members of the Church, but owing to the dissension that existed among them when Dr Philip visited this station,⁴ they were allowed to be no longer members, but Br. Clark considers some of them at present worthy to be returned to Church fellowship.

This place is far from being suitable for a missionary station, on account of the weakness of the spring. At present there is not sufficient water for the cattle, but if there were better management, there would be no want for this purpose, and there might be sufficient to irrigate seven or eight small gardens. This is a decided disadvantage, as but few families will be induced to reside constantly upon the station. The people speak of cultivating land at the different springs scattered about the country. It is most probable that the greatest part of the population will remove from place to place as they have long been in the habit of doing. A system of itineracy will be necessary in order to bring instruction to the whole of the people, and to effect this there ought to be a missionary and schoolmaster belonging to the station.

The population of the place is 20 families of Griquas and about 50 of Bechuannas, who are a kind of refugees from Lattakoo.⁵

1. For Melvill's difficulties at Griquatown, see the letters of Christopher Sass, CWMA 130 (23.5.1826); and Peter Wright, CWMA 132 (30.11.1826).
2. CWMA 136 (8.6.1827).
3. As former Goverment Agent, Melvill was sensitive to this point.
4. In August 1825, when the charges against Goeyman were investigated.
5. Dithakong, to the north of Kuruman, where James Read of the LMS had established a mission in 1816.

The whole population of the country subject to A. Kok amounts to about 60 Griquas and Old Inhabitants together,[6] 150 Bechuannas, 30 Corrannas, and about 30 families of the plundered tribes called Basootoos,[7] making the whole, men, women and children, about 1150.

There are seven clay-built houses belonging to the Old Inhabitants, and five of the same description unfinished. One of these houses is now used as a place of worship and school, which, with another adjoining, is claimed by Jan Goeyman. There is also a square building 20 feet in the sides which was built by the Old Inhabitants at the suggestion of Brother Clark for a place of worship, to be enlarged when convenient. For the present it is used by me as a dwelling house.

The following arrangements have been made made for public worship and instruction for the children. Lord's Day: just after sunrise, prayer meeting; half past nine, forenoon, public service; afternoon, catechetical meeting for children; evening, sermon as in the forenoon. Monday for singing. Tuesday, Wednesday, Thursday and Friday, exposition of Old and New Testament alternately. Saturday, prayer meeting; and first Monday in month, missionary and prayer meeting. School twice every day in the week except Tuesday and Thursday afternoon, catechetical meetings. The usual attendance on the Lord's Day, 25, besides a few children. In the school there are 50, including 15 Bechuannas.[8]

In a report written more than a year later, in June 1828, Melvill gave further details of the settlement.

It is now about two years since this station (originally established for the Bushmen) was given up to the Griquas under the Chief Adam Kok. Shortly after they settled in these parts, the party called Bergenaars (notorious for their plundering excursions in the interior and attacks upon Griqua Town), who had previously put themselves under the authority of this Chief, rebelled and left the country, leaving only about 45 Griqua families and a few Corannas and Bechuanas, who remained faithful. However, since that period the population of the country connected with the station had gradually increased, and at present it is nearly as follows: Griqua families, 120; Coranna do., 210; Bechuana do., including many of the tribes plundered by the Bergenaars, 240; which together is about 2850 men, women and children.

It may be proper to remark that most of the Griquas and some of the Corannas and Bechuanas did at one time or other hear the Gospel before they came to this country, but most of the former, having lived a wandering and unsettled life at a distance from a missionary station for some years past, they have generally speaking retrograded rather than made progress in evangelization and civilization. It will scarcely be credited that all the Griqua women in these parts (with the exception of only about half a dozen) smear and paint their bodies, wear the native dress, and load themselves with beads. In this respect they differ nothing from the Corannas. The men, however, differ in this particular, and without exception wear some kind of clothing,[9] and some are even decently dressed. The Coranna men also very generally wear leather trousers of their own making. Heathenish dancing, with its attendant immorality, is not uncommon, and sorcery is also still occasionally practised among all the tribes in these parts. But notwithstanding the general bad character of the Griquas, if allowance be made for the many natural disadvantages to which they are subject, there are some [*illegible*] persons among them who are no doubt indebted to the introduction of the Gospel among them for their present favourable circumstances, and I do hope

6. Families are obviously meant.
7. See p.27 n9 above.
8. "Only one person can read, two are beginning to read, four or five are spelling. All the rest are beginning the ABC" (note in the margin of the original).—Source of quotation: CWMA 135 (2.4.1827).
9. i.e., some kind of western dress.

there are a few, tho' but a few, to whom the Gospel has been made the power of God to the salvation of their souls. (…)

Of the effects of the Gospel among the people to whom it is preached, it is to be deplored that it is scarcely any evidence of their being benefited by it. There seems to be a general indifference to the things belonging to their everlasting peace, and too many, it is to be feared, despise the day of God's merciful visitation. Some who appeared to be under good impressions and of whom there were good hopes have fallen away on the day of temptation. There are indeed many baptised persons in this country who are in an awful state of backsliding. The Chief, Adam Kok, however, I have the pleasure to say, continues stedfast and supports the mission as that lies in his power. He encourages and exhorts the people to attend the means of grace and to send their children to school, and exerts himself to get a place of worship built.[10] I would beg to crave for him a small testimony of the goodwill of the Society towards him. A small box of carpenter's tools would prove very acceptable, and tend greatly to encourage him.[11]

Some additional information on Philippolis, and on Melvill's work there, may be obtained by means of extracts from his journal during his first months on the station.[12]

19 February 1827. In the evening the commando went out in pursuit of the Bushmen who stole the cattle on the 9th inst. and murdered the herdsman.

20 February. In the forenoon the commando returned with eight Bushmen, including three boys, whom they took prisoners without firing a shot. The forebearance of the Griquas was owing to one of the old inhabitants of the station being with them who was acquainted with the Bushman Chief and called out to him to submit.

21 February. Today the Bushmen received their punishment,

the men 125 lashes and the boys 8 or 10. They confessed having stolen the cattle, but denied having murdered the herdsman. Among these miserable people was a man who formerly lived on this station and appeared to be under good impressions. He acknowledged to Br. Clark that he had gone astray, and he as well as the whole party promised to come and live on the place. It appears that the spring of Philippolis belongs to this Bushman Chief.

Lord's Day, 25 February. A few persons came from And. Pretoros' place to attend worship. On questioning the old man's wife (formerly a deaconess at Bethelsdorp) about the state of her soul, she confessed she was "going backward".[13] I endeavoured to point out to her the danger of such a state and the necessity of going forward if she wished to save her soul. I exhorted her to pray earnestly and perseveringly for grace to help her. It is a common error among Hottentots to judge of their state by the strength of their feelings, with scarcely any reference to good works or outward conduct. An awakened conscience and strong convictions of sin, without any saving change, is often taken for conversion, and having heard a great deal of predestination without understanding it, and whatever be their conduct afterwards, they believe they cannot be lost. I have met with several Hottentots of this character, and fearing this woman (tho' I hope well of her) might have imbibed these erroneous notions, I endeavoured to convince her that the children of God are "called to be holy and without blame before Him in [*illegible*]".—The attend-

---

10. Elsewhere in this letter, Melvill refers to "a place of worship, which was commenced some time ago and carried up 8 feet high".
11. Source: CWMA 144 (1.7.1828).
12. The journal was also published, in a somewhat emended version, in the Transactions of the LMS during January, April, July and October 1828.
13. Andries Pretorius and his wife, Martha Maurits, who were both prominent members of the congregation at Bethelsdorp. He appears to have been living at Boesmansfontein at this stage.

ance today at Worship was 25.—In the afternoon my "maat" Joris arrived with the Bushmen under him,[14] 20 men, women and children, and intended to live here under our protection.[15]

6 March. Part of the Bushmen punished on the 21st ultimo came to live on the station.—I was told today by Joris that one of the Farmers[16] who was here a day or two ago promised him five sheep if he would give him a little girl, one of his relations. He seemed to want my appreciation. I expressed my abhorrence of such an act, and desired him not to do it.

7 March. We were very much annoyed in the evening and part of the night by the heathenish dances of the Bechuannas. These dances, being attended with most abominable practices, have always been prohibited at the missionary stations among the Griquas, and as Dam[17] seems not to take notice of them, it appears to be our duty to urge him to put a stop to them.

8 March. Br. Clark spoke to the Chief about the Bechuanna dances, and a promise was made to speak to them upon the subject. It is to be feared that these Bechuannas, if they remain in this country, will retrograde rather than improve in civilization.[18] In their own country they were partly an agricultural people, but since they have been among the Griquas their whole time is taken up with their cattle. They are in the habit of removing from place to place, and for conveniency have constructed mat huts similar to those of the Corannas.[19]

As there are several Bushman families upon the station, we think it our duty to give them some instruction on the things of God. We have therefore offered the old interpreter Rds17 per month to assist us. He appears rather unwilling, and has promised to give an answer another day.—The number of persons in our catechetical meeting was 39, and among them seven or eight young men. A married woman formerly a member of the Griqua Town church also generally attends. I am encouraged to hope that these exercises will prove a blessing to the souls of the children.—Our plan of catechising is not to oblige the children to learn by rote the answers to the questions as they are in the book. We endeavour by the most simple language to convey to the[ir?] understandings the real sense and meaning of the subject, and use every means of impressing upon them the importance of true religion. This seems to interest the children more than the method of repeating what they seldom understand.[20]— I was astonished at the ignorance of the Chief's son, a lad [of] about 17. He could not say who Jesus Christ was, nor did he know whether he [*Jesus*] had ever been in the world or not.

Lord's Day, 11 March. A consideration of the importance of keeping the Sabbath holy, and the way in which it is usually profaned by Hottentots and even lightly thought of by converts—I preached upon the subject. The study of the sermon did my own heart good. I was strongly impressed with a sense of the great mercy of God to man in the institution of this blessed day.

12 March. Mr Clark and myself were employed today covering the ridge of the church roof with a coat of clay. Mr C. got a few Bechuannas to assist us, he being of opinion that the Griquas are in too bad a spirit to be asked to assist.—I was informed also

14. A Bushman Kaptyn with whom Melvill had established a formal bond of friendship.
15. It must be borne in mind that Philippolis at this stage was still intended to be an "institution" for the Bushmen, and Clark was still trying to gather them around him here.
16. Trekboers from the Cape Colony.
17. Cornelius Kok III was at this time the nominal Kaptyn at Philippolis, his father having resigned in his favour, but Melvill continues to refer to Adam as Kaptyn.
18. "Westernisation" is meant.
19. These huts of woven mats over a pole framework could easily be transported, as opposed to the more permanent rondavel-type houses traditionally built and occupied by the Batswana.
20. "As the Hottentots speak the Dutch language very imperfectly, the catechisms are nearly unintelligible to them" (note in the original text).— The Basters, Griquas and westernised Khoikhoi largely spoke a local dialect of Dutch which was already developing into the Afrikaans language and assuming an identity of its own.

by Br. C. that there was a prejudice in the mind of the Chief against me on account of my former connection with him as Government Agent. Knowing the natural disposition of this people, I was not greatly surprised to hear of this. However, as he behaves very friendly to me, and attends when it is my turn to preach, I pray that God may change his heart and that this evil may be removed. I am afraid, however, that my former situation will prevent my being useful among the Griquas.

14 March. As some of the Counsellors expressed to Br. Clark their dissatisfaction at my being here as missionary, I took an opportunity of speaking to the Chief upon the subject. I told him I was only here pro tempore and might shortly be removed to another station, and hoped in the mean time we should live in peace and friendship. He confessed he had told Br. C. that he thought on account of my former situation it would not be proper for me to be their missionary, but had not the least objection for me to be here pro tempore, and also added that for his own part he felt nothing in his heart against me.

15 March. In the afternoon a commando went out against some Bushmen who had stolen three head of cattle and murdered the herdsman.

17 March. The commando having returned home, one of the party gave me the following account. Having followed the footmarks of the Bushmen, they came upon the kraal, and found part of the meat, but the inhabitants had fled to a covert of thick reeds. They were followed and surrounded, and many means used to induce them to deliver themselves up, but no answer was given. Some shots were then fired, and it appears one of the Bushmen was killed, upon which the only two that remained made a most determined resistance, talking and swearing in the Dutch language at the Griquas, until at last they were shot with two women and two children that were with them. As eight sleeping places (for they had no huts) had been observed in the kraal, it is concluded that several persons belonging to it escaped and were not discov[er]ed.[21] The Bushmen were no doubt deserters from the Colony.[22] It is not to be wondered at that these people would not give themselves up, for the usual method pursued by the commandoes against them must leave them ignorant of such a thing as giving quarter. O, when will the time come to favour this wretched people?

Lord's Day, 18 March. Preached upon the New Birth. The attendance was very encouraging —there were about 80, including a few Bushmen and Bechuannas, who I regretted could not understand me, and the interpreter did not appear willing to engage. In the catechetical meeting there were 60 children, besides four married women.

19 March. Looking over the Cape paper I see a traveller has attempted to point out the superiority of the system of missionary labour at Lattakoo compared with that at Griqua Town. He thinks he honours the missionaries when he says, "all attempts at conversion are withheld", and thinks it would have been well if the same system had been long ago resorted to and persevered in at the latter place.[23] How little regard these travellers have to truth, and how incapable they are of judging in these matters. I believe no missionaries can be more earnest for the conversion of the people among whom they labour than those of Lattakoo. In a letter I have just received from Br. Moffat he manifests interest in the conversion of sinners. He says, "May the Lord in His infinite mercy prosper you in the glorious work in inviting sinners to the Lamb of God. May the Lord make you not only faithful but

21. The "sleeping places" were hollows in the ground marking improvised camping sites of the Bushmen.
22. The meaning is presumably that they had removed from the Colony under the pressure of white expansion.
23. There was considerable rivalry between the missions at Kuruman ("Lattakoo") and Griquatown, and a degree of enmity between their respective missionaries, Robert Moffat and Peter Wright, Wright being a loyal supporter of Dr Philip, while Moffat and his wife were highly critical of him.

fruitful in His vineyard." With respect to Lattakoo he adds, "Here alas! it is still hope against hope. But He who has promised will surely perform. That God can of the very stones raise up children to Abraham is a promise which often raises my spirits. The Lord's arm is not shortened nor His ear heavy, and He will yet answer us by terrible things in righteousness." "I intend to proceed alone to some place in the interior to preach and improve in the language."

20 March. Today the Chief and Council came to a resolution to build a place of worship.

21 March. The foundation of the chapel was dug. It is 56 by 18 feet, to be attached to the building that I live in. This is perhaps a beginning of good things. Of late there seems to be a great change for the better in the spirit of the Chief. Some time ago the people in general were talking about settling at the different springs about the country, and it was supposed that not more than five families would reside upon the station. Perhaps the things going on at Griqua Town has [*sic*] had some influence and provoked them to jealousy.[24] O that it may be more than a zeal for outward things. May God have mercy upon their souls and convert them from the error of their ways.

22 March. About 30 persons were employed bringing stones from an adjoining hillock for the place of worship.

24 March. I was informed by Mr Clark that the prejudice against me was again manifested by some of the Counsellors. Fearing that my remaining here against the wishes of the people might be injurious to the mission, and Mr Miles[25] having advised me to remove from among the Griquas if I observed a prejudice against me, I resolved to leave the place and go to Graaf Reinet, and remain there until I receive further instructions from Mr Miles.

25 March, Lord's Day. In the afternoon three of the Old Inhabitants called upon me and expressed their regret that I intended to leave the station. One of them observed that two children only were the cause of the opposition. By "children" he meant young persons, whom I could understand to be Dam's son Cornelius and his son-in-law Hendrik Hendriks.[26] Being the Lord's Day, I endeavoured to turn the subject to a spiritual use. They all acknowledged (but I suppose they chiefly alluded to the Griquas) that they had so long slighted the privileges they enjoyed and the mercy of God that they should not wonder if the Gospel were removed from them altogether and they were left to the horrors of their native darkness and heathenism.[27]

26 March. Last night a council was held upon the subject of my leaving the place, and this morning the Chief and Counsellors requested to speak to Br. Clark and me. We met in the church, and the Chief expressed his surprise and regret that I intended to leave them, having supposed that after we had spoken together all old differences had been settled. He said it was his wish that I should remain here until I was appointed to another station. Some of the Counsellors who spoke expressed themselves to the same effect. I endeavoured to convince them that I was not activated by any ill-will against any person, but hearing that a prejudice existed against me which might be followed by disagreeable consequences, I thought it was better to depart in peace. The Chief seemed to want to avoid entering into explanation[28] upon the alleged opposition, but assured me that he had nothing in his heart against me, [and] charged me to consent to remain. I told him I

24. Probably a reference to a revival or resurgence of religious zeal at Griquatown.
25. The Acting Superintendent of the LMS during Philip's absence.
26. Cornelius Kok III, the nominal Kaptyn at ths time (see n17 above); and Hendrick Hendrickze, later Secretary to the Griqua Raad, was a former Bergenaar who still engaged in raiding activities and was not particularly well disposed towards the missionaries (see the journal entry for 5 April below). The two men were both about 30 years old.
27. "What a useful lesson to professing Christians in this country!" added the editor of the Transactions in a footnote to the edited version of Mellvill's journal published there.
28. "Knowing perhaps that his sons were the persons opposed to me" (marginal note in the original).

would take it into consideration, but this did not satisfy them. They followed me to my house, and pressed me to give them an answer. Having reason to believe that they were sincere, and that the prejudice against me was confined to a few individuals, I made up my mind to remain, but deferred giving an answer until the next morning.

27 March. Went this morning to the Chief and told him of my intention to remain, at which he seemed pleased and offered to assist me in any way that laid [*sic*] in his power. I took the opportunity of urging him to send to Campbell for slates, that the children might be taught to write and cypher, which he promised to do.—The people were actively employed today under the superintendence of the Chief in building the place of worship.— The two or three persons who were said to have been opposed to me were particularly friendly.

Lord's Day, 1 April. There was a pretty good and attentive congregation today. In the afternoon there were 72 in the catechetical meeting, including a few adults. On account of a report that the Caffres intended to attack the place the evening meeting was held before sunset. There is general expectation among the people that the Caffre tribes who were plundered by the Bergenaars will revenge themselves on the inhabitants of this country.[29]

2 April. Spoke to the Chief about his soul. He confessed he had been going astray, but said he felt a pleasure in hearing the Word of God. From all that he said I hope he is in a fair way of recovery from a backsliding state.

5 April. Had some serious conversation with Klein Hendrik, the Chief's son-in-law,[30] about his soul. This man was a member of the church at Griqua Town, and can read and write. He fell into sin, and became one of the leading men of the Bergenaars. He seemed to be deeply confinced[?][31] of the sinfulness of his former life, and scarcely thought it possible that there was forgiveness for him. He felt so much that he trembled exceedingly and could hardly speak. He compared himself to to the dog returned to his vomit,[32] and, believing him to be under strong convictions of conscience, I exhorted him to return unto his offended God with full purpose of heart like the Prodigal Son and throw himself into the arms of Mercy.

9 April. My wife commenced a sewing school. She regretted that she could not take more than six children, not having work to employ more for the present.

10 April. The Chief and his Council held a consultation with Br. Clark and me upon the subject of removing the mission to a more eligible situation on account of the want of sufficient water at this place. We both agreed in opinion that it was not fit for an Oorlam station,[33] as no gardens could be made, and approved of the proposal of the Chief to examine Grootfontein, 10 miles northwest of this, and if it was found a suitable place we would write to the Society's Agent at Cape Town for his sanction to the alteration.

13 April. Today three or four families came from the outposts to live upon the station. We have not about 95 children in the school, and expect an increase. Our school house is too small. There are now 27 Griqua families and 3 of the Old Inhabitants and 50 Bechuanna families residing on the station. More are expected, but the small quantity of water for the cattle I am afraid will deter some from coming.[34]

In the circumstances itinerating formed an important part of the pastoral work of a missionary at Philippolis, and Melvill's

29. The reference here may be either to scattered amaXhosa in the Orange River area or to Sotho-Tswana refugees.
30. Hendrik Hendrickze.
31. Transcribed as "convinced" in the published version of the journal.
32. A biblical reference.
33. i.e., for a station for a (semi-)westernised people such at the Griquas or Basters who practised agriculture.
34. Source: CWMA Journals 1592.

journal also includes an account of his travels among the scattered families and other groups and tribes who had settled at the fountains in the district.

22 June [1827]. Being desirous that the Corannas who submitted to our Chief should come to the station that I might conveniently visit them,[35] I resolved to go out and speak to them upon the subject. I accordingly sent out from Philippolis for this purpose at 11 in the morning. Arrived at night at the *werf* of Piet Sabba, formerly native teacher at Ramah.[36] This *werf* consists of 12 Griqua and 17 Bechuana families. The latter are mostly of the Bashootoo tribe who were plundered by the Bergenaars. From the accounts given by these people they were driven from their native country by a tribe of Caffres whom they call Matabeele, which is probably the Tambookies. After this they were attacked and intirely impoverished by the Bergenaars, whom they followed into this country. Many hundreds have since found their way to many parts of the Colony.[37] Who can tell whether some of these people may not become acquainted with the Great Salvation and be the means of introducing it among the tribes in the interior?— Only about 8 Griquas attended my evening service.

23 June. This forenoon preached to about 15 Griquas. It is very much to be regretted that no suitable interpreter can be found for the Bechuannas who are so numerous in these parts. Departed at 10 a.m., and arrived at 1/2 past at Kalk Fountain.[38] This is the farm of the Chief's son Cornelius. He is employed making a dam for collecting the water to irrigate some ground which he and some other people want to cultivate.

I met with a man here who gave me great cause of rejoicing and encouragement. His name is Diedrik, the brother of Kobus Flermuis of Namaqualand. He was my driver to Griqua Town, and appears to have received some good impression on the road.[39] He was taken ill soon after his return, and is just recovering, tho' still confined by a lameness in his legs. He informs me that he felt seriously concerned about his soul many years ago when he heard the Gospel at Griqua Town, but having gone to Namaqualand, the impressions soon wore off, and he afterwards lived in great wickedness. It is some years since he returned to this country. During his late illness he seems to have been under conviction of sin and to have felt the importance of attending to the salvation of his soul. He says he prayed earnestly and constantly, and at last felt as if a great weight was taken off his breast, meaning that he felt that his sins were pardoned. He said he had resigned himself into the hands of God and is indifferent whether he lives or dies.

Altho' he could not express himself in a clear manner from his imperfect knowledge of the Dutch language and from being unaccustomed to speak on religious subjects, I have reason to think from the answers he gave to some questions I put to him that the merits of Christ are the foundation upon which he builds his hopes of acceptance with God. Time must prove the genuineness of the work. If it be of God it will stand, and the gates of Hell will not prevail against it. Charity hopeth all things, and this grace is much called for among poor heathen who labour under

35. This casual phrase reveals much about the attitude of the early missionaries to the objects of their labours: the convenience of the Korana themselves was obviously not a consideration.
36. "Werf is used by the Griquas in the same sense as kraal, wherever they pitch their tents or mat huts the place is called the werf" (marginal note in the original).
37. A brief account of the Difaqane, a series of violent upheavals on the Highveld in the 1820s, seemingly initiated by the invasion of Nguni tribes from beyond the Drakensberg who were known locally as "Matabele", and are not to be confused with the amaNdebele of Mzilikazi. The "Tambookies" were amaThembu, a distinct Nguni tribe.
38. Kalkfontein on the Orange River. This and Ramah were the chief "werfs" or settlements in the Philippolis Captaincy.
39. This presumably refers to Melvill's journey from Cape Town to Griquatown in 1822; the "good impression" would have been religious.—Cobus Vlermuis was a well-known raider, mentioned by the missionary Hodgson in 1823 as "the famous Cobus"; Hodgson, p.193.

many disadvantages. By their fruits, however, shall we be able to discover the children of God from the children of the Devil. For the present, being willing to hope the best of this man, it seems proper to nourish the apparent good impressions, and pray to God that if He has begun a good work, to perform it until the day of Christ. O that this may be the beginning of a time of refreshing from His presence, may be the few drops before an abundant shower of divine grace poured out upon this dry and barren land, that it may rejoice and blossom as the rose.

I was much gratified to find the children, about 17 in number, anxious to return to school. I heard their lessons, and after I had finished, it was pleasant to see them sit down and teach others.—In the evening preached to about 17 persons.

24 June, Lord's Day. A Dutch farmer (of whom there are several about the country, having been permitted to come over the Zwart River [40] on account of the great drought) paid me a visit and attended our public service in the fornenoon. From his conversation he appeared to be more than a so-called Christian. He belongs to Graaf Reinet district, and spoke very highly of the minister, Revd Mr Murray, who has dealt faithfully with his soul.[41]—I sent word to some Farmers in the neighbourhood of my institution of my intention to hold service, and invited them to attend. They asked the messenger whether I would preach in the open air and whether I did not come for the Hottentots, to which the man replied, "The Word is free for all." They then promised to come if they found their horses,[42] but never made their appearance.

25 June. Expounded 1 chapter of John's First Epistle to Diedrik and exhorted him to continue in the grace of God.—Had some conversation with a man who was baptised about twelve years ago at Griqua Town, but who had departed from the Truth. He seems to see the error of his ways, and to be making some feeble resolves to "arise and go to his Father". I endeavoured to convince him of the infinite compassion of the God whom he had offended, and of His willingness to heal backsliders.

26 June. Piet Sabba, whom I engaged to accompany as interpreter, having arrived, I rode away early in the morning, and arrived just after dark near the place where we supposed to meet with the Corannas. Saw several fires not far off which we concluded to be Farmers, but could not proceed on account of the badness of the road. Halted for the night near the Zwart River.

27 June. The morning light discovered to us that we were near some Farmers, and a Coranna kraal was seen a quarter of an hour beyond them. As soon as the oxen were brought (having been allowed to graze in the night), we spanned in, and reached the Corannas at 9 a.m. The head of the werf is Abraham Kruger, son of a Dutch Farmer by a Coranna woman.[43] There are 21 Coranna and 6 Bechuanna huts.—Owing to the cold wind that blew, and having service in the open air, could only get 12 men to attend. The present season of the year, being often very cold, is unfavourable for itinerating. I never felt so much the want of a good tent as today—it would have approved a convenient place of worship.—I spoke to Kruger about removing nearer to the station and the importance of the children been taught to read and writing. He said he was very anxious for the children to go to school, and wished to settle at a fountain in the neighbourhood of Philippolis where he might make a garden.—One of the Farmers who lay near the Corannas called and requested me to go and stop at his post on my return to preach, which I promised to do.—In the afternoon nearly all the men went out hunting.—In the evening, on account of the cold and in the hopes of having

40. The Orange.
41. Andrew Murray Sr, a Scottish-born minister, who had succeeded Abraham Faure at Graaff-Reinet in 1822.
42. In the absence of fences, horses and oxen often strayed while grazing, and on occasion several days might be required to find them.
43. The last phrase was omitted in the published version of the journal. Abraham Kruger was a well-known raider in the area, and one of the men Dr Philip had met on the Riet River in August 1825.

more hearers than in the morning, held service in Kruger's hut, which is of hemispherical form, 12 feet diameter. 23 persons crowded into it, and some sat outside.

28 June. It was my intention to have visited some other Coranna kraals lower down the river, but one of my oxen having become lame, and there being no proper wagon road and the country very rugged, resolved to return home. Rode to the farmers in the forenoon, and preached from Luke 7:50. After the service one of the Farmers' wives spoke very freely upon religion in a manner that gave me reason to hope that she experiences the love of God in her soul.—In the evening rode a few miles up the river to the Coranna werf of Old Philip.[44] This kraal consists of 11 families, besides Bechuanna servants. Preached to about 20 persons sitting round the fire.

9 June. Preached in the forenoon to about 25 persons, mostly females; nearly all the men had gone out hunting.—In a conversation with Old Philip he said he was heartily tired of roving about, and would come and settle at Philippolis or at a fountain near it.—Departed at 1 p.m., and arrived at Kalk Fontein (*30 June*) early in the morning. In the afternoon I instructed the children, and preached in the evening to about 15 hearers.

1 July, Lord's Day. Had service forenoon, afternoon and evening, and school for the children. Spoke to Diedrik from Col. 3.[45] He seems determined by the grace of God to follow the Lord. He told me that having awoke suddenly last night he called out to his wife, "When will the day come that we shall all say, Begone world, begone, sin." These words are part of a hymn which he had heard in former days. He mentioned this with evident feeling, and expressed his hope that he might be enabled to act up to the meaning of the words.—I was anxious to take some of the children with me to Philippolis, as they are so desirous to return to school, but their parents assured me that it was out of their power to support them at the station.

2 July. Left Kalk Fontein at sunrise, and arrived at Philippolis a little before sunset.

5 July. Rode on horseback to a Griqua kraal, and preached to about 25 persons. I spoke to them about sending their children to school. They said they were anxious for the children to be taught, but as the cows were nearly all dried up and they had nothing else to subsist upon, it was impossible to send the children for the present. One of them urgently requested me to take his two sons into my family.

6 July. In consequence of the Landdrost's plan of giving cattle to the Bushmen, 66 men, women and children have arrived.[46] It is remarkable that there is not one child to each family, there being only 17 to about 25 families. This is probably owing to several being in the service of the Farmers, though indeed the few children generally found among Bushmen may also be accounted for from their hard life and insufficient subsistence, and from their sometimes practising infanticide.

8 July, Lord's Day. A few persons from the outstations attended the public service. —In the evening had an agreeable conversation with the Chief. He spoke with much feeling of his former state of backsliding, which was occasioned by his leaving the means of grace[47] at Griqua Town and living at his cattle post. At present I have reason to think that his soul is restored, and that he really enjoys religion.

9 July. Commenced a meeting[48] for five Griqua women, two of whom I hope are truly pious and the others somewhat con-

---

44. Philip and his Korana are mentioned as living at the Orange-Vaal junction in 1786, downstream from Hardcastle (modern Douglas) in 1813, and at Philippolis in 1829.
45. Colossians (New Testament).
46. This refers to a plan conceived by Andries Stockenstrom for settling the Bushmen.
47. The religious services and sacraments.
48. "This meeting is to be held weekly, and is intended to give instructions to the persons who attend applicable to the state of their minds, and occasionally to hear their experience" (marginal note in the original).

cerned about their souls. Four of the members were baptised many years ago, but appeared to have wandered far away from the paths of peace, as is the case with many in this country. The wanderings of these people from the ways of God may be generally traced up their leaving the missionary stations. They often do it from necessity in dry seasons, but too often, it is so be feared, they neglect to return when it is in their power, and not hearing the Word of God for a considerable time, the impression of divine things may be naturally expected to wear off.[49] This state of things points out the absolute necessity for itinerating in order to insure success in the missionary work, and for this purpose there ought to be two missionaries belonging to a station. And as itinerating is often attended with inconveniences, it should be a duty positively insisted upon, to prevent the temptation of loving home more than is expedient.

11 July. Made an attempt today to speak to the Bechuannas by means of my Mantatee boy.[50] The men were at work in an inclosure preparing skins and making karosses. I told them my object in coming was to speak to them about the things of God, and requested them to leave off working for a few minutes. It was with evident reluctance that they sat to hear me.[51] Indifference was evident in their countenances while I spoke of the things that concerned their everlasting peace. I was inclined to say, Can these dry bones live? How can such people become converted to God who have no idea of futurity or that they possess immortal souls, and can form no idea of happiness or misery beyond the grave? The only answer to these evil suggestions tending to discourage exertions is, [*illegible*] He that commanded light to shine out of darkness can when He pleases enlighten their dark minds and give them the light of the knowledge of the glory of God in the face[?] of Jesus Christ.

13 July. Had 62 children in the school this afternoon. 26 were Bechuannas and 8 Bushmen, and the rest Griquas, 6 of the latter adults.

15 July, Lord's Day. Had a tolerably good congregation, several persons having come from the outposts.

21 July. A field cornet and two other persons belonging to the Colony arrived. The object [*illegible*] was to distribute 49 head of cattle among the Bushmen.

22 July, Lord's Day. The field cornet gave the cattle to the Bushmen and put them under the protection of the Chief of this place. The strangers attended my forenoon service, and rode away in the afternoon. I gave each of them a few Dutch tracts.

25 July. Visited the Bechuannas. Endeavoured to enter into conversation about eternal things, but found great difficulty in getting them to hear me. As they are generally at work during the day time, I proposed to have a meeting for them in the evening once a week, which they promised to attend. About 40, old and young, attended in the place of worship, and appeared attentive.—Today I commenced a meeting for a few baptised [people][52] who I hope are not without the grace of God. It is to be conducted in the same manner as that for the women. The reason for having separate meetings is that there may [be?] less reserve in expressing the state of their minds.—I was happy to hear that the Chief had commenced family worship, which had been given up for many years.

8 August. Rode to Kalk Fountain. Preached in the evening to 15 persons.

9 August. Preached morning, afternoon and evening. Had about 20 to 25 hearers each time. The attention of the people at this place is very encouraging.

49. That is, in the way of (human) nature.
50. His male Tlokwa servant or attendant
51. In fairness to the Batswana is should be remembered that their visitor had intruded himself upon them unasked.
52. "People" is taken from the printed text, which omits the remainder of the passage on this subject; the original word, scored through in the manuscript, seems from the context to have been "men".

10 August. Conversed with a few persons who seem to have some concern about their souls.—Rode away at 1 p.m., and stopped for the night at Piet Sabba's werf. Had only 6 persons. The people at this place are the most indifferent of any of the Griquas to concerns of their souls, and it is not improbable that the contact and example of Piet Sabba, formerly a native preacher, has brought religion into disesteem among the people who have been living with him.

11 August. Departed at sunrise, and reached Philippolis in the afternoon.[53]

As a result of the inadequacy of the fountain at Philippolis regularly referred to in accounts of the station, the Griqua Raad decided early in 1829 that the settlement should be moved to the nearby Boesmansfontein, but there was a good deal of opposition to the move, especially on the part of the Old Inhabitants, who had been living here for some years and had built houses for themselves. By the beginning of October only Melvill and the family of Adam Kok II had removed to the new site,[54] and it would seem that the decision was ultimately not implemented, with the result that Philippolis itself, for lack of an adequate water supply, never developed to any notable extent, and Melvill had to continue spending a great deal of his time in itinerating.

There does not appear to be any reason to doubt the sincerity of Melvill's missionary vocation or of his desire to help the Griquas, considering the sacrifices he made for these causes, but sincerity is unfortunately no guarantee of success. By 1831, when he had already been working at Philippolis for four years, even the Annual Report of the LMS could offer no very encouraging information on the results of his labours, although it was compiled from the reports of the missionaries themselves on a highly selective basis, with a view to presenting the most favourable picture of their activities possible to the world at large.

Though many unfavourable circumstances have tried the patience and faith of the missionary who is placed at this station, he has hitherto persevered in the discharge of his important and arduous duties. Early in last year [*1830*] abundant rains began, after a long drought, to water the parched ground. When this had taken place, several families removed nearer to the station, and sent their children to school. The attendance of the services on the Sabbath began to improve, varying from 80 to 200; and in the school Mr Melvill had the gratification to see from 45 to 80 children. The spirit of the people appeared generally improved, and Mr Melvill indulges the hope that the Lord may yet more abundantly bless his labours among the people.

Secular affairs. The general population amounts to 1860 persons, of whom 900 are Griquas and 960 Bechuanas. These people are dispersed over a large tract of country, the land being chiefly adapted to grazing. The number of those who actually reside at the station varies considerably at different times of the year.

At Philippolis there is a chapel, a mission house, and storehouse and twelve dwelling houses. The land lately brought under cultivation comprehends about 280 acres, which is irrigated from 50 fountains. The Griquas prefer gardening to raising corn, and besides a variety of vegetables cultivated, they have in some gardens planted the peach, the fig tree and the vine.[55]

In October 1830, after his return to England, Richard Miles, who supplied Dr Philip's place during the latter's protracted absence, compiled an official survey of the work of the LMS in

---

53. Source: CWMA Journals 1592.
54. "The Chief with his son-in-law H[endrik] H[endricks}, the widow of his late son Cornelius, and his wife's mother and families"; CWMA 153 (29.10.1829).
55. Source: Report (1831), pp.88–89.

South Africa in which he remarked, "Mr Melvill has diligently exerted himself at this station for the general improvement of the people since the removal of Mr Clark, and for a considerable time the prospects were very encouraging, but the subsequent unsettled state of the Griquas has considerably changed the aspect of affairs".[56]

One of the main factors militating against the success of Melvill's work at Philippolis, as he had already noted himself in his earliest journal entries on the station, was that considerable prejudice existed against him among the Griqua section of the community on account of the political role he had played in the affairs of Griquatown as official Agent of the Cape Government. This does not seem to have changed with the passage of time, and in connection with the proposed removal to Boesmansfontein he could make the following entries in his journal.

Tuesday, 13th [October 1829]. Entered into conversation with the Chief about the removal of the station. He said some of the people were opposed to it upon the ground that they had paid for the houses at Old Philippolis. From some remarks the old man made, it appeared that he was inclined to favour this opinion. This subject being dropped, he told me he had spoken to the people about their not coming to live at the station, and put the question to them (agreeably to my request) whether there existed any prejudice against me, and if that was the cause of it. To this question only two of the Counsellors made any reply, and they had no reason to be prejudiced—the rest were silent. The Chief remarked that he suspected that their silence implies something unfavourable, adding that his wife had told him that one Fortuin Kok[57] had said that he had not been consulted when I was chosen as their missionary, and that I was the Chief's missionary but not his, and that some other persons were of his opinion.

The Chief stated further that there was a genuine dissatisfaction on account of my not having brought a good supply of gunpowder for the people, knowing as I did their difficulties and wants,[58] that two other missionaries had brought some for the Chiefs with whom they were connected, and that I should have done the same; the people therefore thought I did not take an interest in their welfare, and that he for his part could not in conscience traffic in the dark and thus procure gunpowder in an unlawful manner, but wished to get it openly.

I replied to the Chief that he acted very right in following the dictates of his conscience, and that I was obliged to do the same. Gunpowder was a contraband article, and therefore, whatever other missionaries did, my conscience could not allow me to transgress the law, that I had used what means were in my power to enable him to procure this article from Government in a lawful manner, and that was all I could do. With these and some other remarks which I made he seemed to be satisfied, but there is reason to fear the unfavourable impression made upon the minds of the people, who cannot enter into my motives, will not be soon effaced. However, I cannot purchase their goodwill by a sacrifice of principle.[59]

In a letter to London written in February 1830, a few months later, Melvill reverted to this specific complaint against him, and to further developments arising from it.

You will no doubt have heard of the unfavourable state of things at this station up to the date of my letter (29 October) to Mr

---

56. CWMA 165 (27.10.1830).
57. "This man was one of the Bergenaars and had asked me for some gunpowder a short time ago, which I could not give him, and therefore gave him offence" (note in the original).
58. As Agent at Griquatown Melvill had been empowered by the Cape authorities to supply the people with gunpowder.
59. Source: CWMA 153 (29.10.1829).

Miles. If that letter (which contained extracts from my journal) reached you, you will have seen that when I was enjoying some hopes of improvements, very unexpectedly an unpleasant feeling was excited against me on account of my not having brought a supply of gunpowder for the people, which they had been led to expect from my having formerly supplied the Chief of Griqua Town with that article. I was also informed at the same time that a direct prejudice existed against me on account of my former situation as Government Agent.

Not doubting the truth of this assertion, I could not help thinking that this circumstance had operated against my usefulness among this people. I was in consequence induced to suggest to Mr Miles that it might be proper under those circumstances to to remove me to another field of labour. From a letter I lately received from Dr Philip (into whose hands my letter to Mr Miles was put on his arrival at the Cape),[60] I am sorry to say my suggestion has been construed into an application to be removed to the Colony, which is a most erroneous construction of my words.[61]

After Philip's return to the Cape, he was once more able to give his personal attention to the problems of the Northern Frontier, and as his plans om this regard grew more ambitious, he became increasingly concerned about the situation at Philippolis. During the course of 1830 therefore, by his own account, he informed Melvill "that I had no objection to remove him into the Colony, provided he would become a schoolmaster, and wholly devote himself to the business of teaching".[62] Early the following year Melvill—somewhat, it would seem, to his own surprise—found himself transferred to Hankey in the Eastern Cape, and in March 1831 he was succeeded at Philippolis by G.A. Kolbe, Clark's assistant at Bushman Station.

A particularly detailed account of the condition of Philippolis, both as a settlement and as a mission station, four years after Melvill's arrival there, is provided by the official returns for the station as on 18 January 1831, which he sent to London on the eve of his departure. The following is a précis of the printed form completed by him.

Name of station or out-station: Philippolis.
Missionaries: 1
Day schools: 1. The children receive religious instruction three times a week.
Average number of congregation: on Sabbath, first, 50 to 140;[63] on week days, 30 to 50
Present number of candidates for baptism: 1 female; candidates for communion, 6 females.
Number the place of worship will seat and hold: 200. A new building is being erected.
Population belonging to the station:
At station, Griquas: 6 males,[64] 10 females, 16 children; Bechuanas: 120
Outposts, Griquas: 868; Bechuanas: 840
Connected with station: total, 1860. The population of the station is rapidly increasing.
Cattle and implements, belonging to the Griquas: 362 horses; 4550 oxen, cows and calves;14 200 sheep and goats; 45 wagons; 15 ploughs.
Belonging to the Bechuanas: 2100 oxen, cows and calves; 1200 sheep and goats.
Land and houses: the territory in possession of the Griqua in connection with this station, though the boundaries have not been correctly defined,[65] comprehend about 3000 square miles, of which about 350 are capable of cultivation. At the station there are about 42 acres which are cultivated.
State of cultivation:
Sown or planted—wheat: owing to the ravages of the locusts, one half of the of the corn was destroyed, yet 750 bushels were harvested this last season; oats: none; barley, 60 bushels. Maize, beans, potatoes, peas, carrots, beet, onions, pumpkins have been sown and planted in abundance.

60. Philip returned to the Cape in October 1829.
61. Source: CWMA 155 (4.2.1830).
62. CWMA 167 (14.1.1831).
63. Presumably the first Sunday in the month is meant.
64. In the original the statistics here are broken down into "married", "unmmarried" and "widowers", and similarly under other headings.
65. It will be remembered that Melvill had been a land surveyor.

Number of trees—400

Money distributed for public objects: 75 goats and sheep and 9 cows and heifers were contributed for the Bushman Station.

Form of return for missionary families:
Missionary: John Melvill, age 43
His wife, Anna Frederica, age 35
Children: Thomas John, 17; Wilhelmina Elizabeth, 14; Jennet, 11; John George, 8; Helen Edward, 6; Anna, 4; Samuel, 2
Miscellaneous observations: It will be observed how small a proportion of the station are resident upon the station. This may be partly accounted for from the desultory habits of the people, but is also owing to a great part of the population being settled upon their own farms, and many others, whose only means of subsistence are derived fom their cattle, are absolutely obliged, at least at certain seasons of the year, to roam about in search of pasturage. During part of the year, however, a number of families take up a temporary residence upon the station. At present more people come from the outposts on the Lord's Day to attend the means of grace than at any former period.—As the harvest has just been got in, I expect the population of the station and the number of children in the school will be increased.[66]

66. Source: CWMA 164.—It should be pointed out that Melvill's successor, G.A.Kolbe, filling in the same official printed form only nine months later, gave widely differing figures, e.g. (under the heading "Cattle and implements") 1000 oxen, 3000 calves and calves, 50 000 sheep, 5000 goats, 160 wagons and 20 ploughs (CWMA 170). The two missionaries may have been using different standards of assesssment, but it seems probable that Melvill would have been the more accurate observer.

4.
G.A. Kolbe (1831–1836)

George Augustus Kolbe, an Englishman by birth, and his wife Margaret had come out to South Africa with the 1820 Settlers, on which occasion he had given his age as 20, though he was in fact 17, and his profession as apothecary. From 1823 to 1827 he worked as a missionary among the slaves in the Graaff-Reinet district, but when the local missionary society, by whom he was employed, was taken over by the LMS, he transferred his services to the latter body, and was placed by Richard Miles at Bushman Station with Clark.[1] He was paid £25 a year, being a basic salary of £100 with an additional £5 for each child, but he seems to have had private means, for he later claimed never to have drawn his full salary.[2]

It is not clear why Dr Philip subsequently saw fit to transfer this relatively inexperienced young man, who was not ordained and who seems to have been unknown to him personally, to Philippolis, which he was increasingly beginning to regard as the keystone in his grand plan for the interior of South Africa.

Kolbe arrived at Philippolis with his family on 13 March 1831: he was 28 years of age, as was his wife, and they had five

1. For Kolbe, see CWMA 144 (Richard Miles, 7.6.1828); CWMA 150 (Certificate of Ds. Andrew Murray, 2.4.1829).—For the proposed union of the Graaff-Reinet Missionary Society and the LMS, see CWMA 145 ("Rules of proposed union...", July? 1828); ibid. (R. Miles, 8.8.1828); CWMA 151 (R. Miles, 17.7.1829).
2. See p.89 below.

children, the eldest of whom was eight and the youngest about one month old. To the Auxiliary Mission Society of the LMS in Cape Town he supplied an extremely enthusiastic description of his new station for their annual report, on which they commented as follows.[3]

About the beginning of March [1831] Mr Kolbe, who had for some time laboured among the Bushmen on the Caledon River, removed to this place, and the Lord soon approved to bless his labours among the people. In July he writes, "I have the greatest pleasure in informing you that the work of the Lord is greatly progressing here. A great revival of religion has visibly taken place, and many who have been living without God in the world are now anxiously asking the way. There are now 20 candidates for baptism and church fellowship. The church is continually filled, and from 170 to 200 persons constantly attend divine service.[4] I have at present 84 children in the school, and we are going on tolerably well with the building of our new church. At the last missionary prayer meeting I requested the people to subscribe for the Society, and they came voluntarily after the service and subscribed in the amount of Rds [*rixdollars*] 100. The good work proceeded, and another and another was brought to a concern for their immortal interests, and several that had formerly made a profession of religion were led to see the sinfulness of their conduct in having forsaken God, and to return with weeping and supplications unto the Lord. The congregation increased so much that the place of worship would not contain them, and they were obliged at times to erect a temporary tent to screen those that were outside from the sun. The attendance on the week evening meetings was doubled. The children at the school often amounted to 100, and 7 persons were admitted to the Lord's Supper."

For October Mr Kolbe writes to Dr Philip, "It is with the greatest pleasure that I reply to yours of the 10th August [1831], and am still the more happy to be able to say that the work of the Lord is increasing. Your kind letter I read to the Church, and I can assure you that it made my heart and the hearts of all the disciples of Jesus glad. Last Sabbath I was highly delighted in finding that a lost of [?] flock had [?]. Many Corannas are come to this station desiring to hear the Word of God, and acknowledging their [?] sins and desiring to return to the fold of Christ.

"As we are bound to supply the workmen of our new church, who gratuitously give their labour, with daily food, our stock of provisions was quite exhausted, but I informed the children who attend the school that I intended to send a paper round the village for subscriptions to the church. Ere it left the schoolroom, nine sheep were subscribed, and a goat by a Bechuana who has but a few of these animals to depend on for subsistence. In the course of an hour, although but a few families were on the place, it being the middle of the week, 16 sheep were subscribed. Some assistance from Cape Town[5] would be of essential service, and above all things it would convince the people here that they met with encouragement from their fellow-Christians.

"I have frequently been necessitated since my arrival at the station to seek a place of retirement, in order to weep tears of gratitude and to offer up my thanksgivings to Almighty God for what He has wrought amongst us. May the Lord continue to bless His own work and therefore dear. To add fuel to the flames, give us your prayers and your advice. You do all in your power to help us. Oh, may conscience never upbraid us that we have

---

3. This comment was not published by the Society, but the text of an edited version has been preserved in the archives of the LMS.
4. It will be remembered that Melvill, in the return submitted six months earlier, had stated that church attendance was between 50 and 140 on Sundays. The disparity between the figures, if correct, may well be seen as a measure of Melvill's unpopularity in the community
5. I.e., from the Auxiliary Missionary Society there.

done the work of the Lord negligently, knowing that there is a reward according to our works."[6]

A somewhat more realistic account of Kolbe's labours on the station is provided by the first section of the journal he forwarded to London.

6 November [1831], Sunday. 260 persons attended the different services of religion today. Three candidates were admitted as church members. In the evening the Lord's Supper was administered to 15 persons. After the sacrament two persons came to me desiring to speak about their spiritual state before God.[7]

7 November. 100 persons attended the missionary prayer meeting.

9 November. The Chief sent a letter to the Veld Cornet Joubert[8] complaining of the intrusions of the Farmers, especially of the Colonists, who had insulted and beaten his people.

20 November, Sunday. 178 persons attended the services. Proclaimed a solemn fast to the Lord for the acknowledgment of sin and deprecating His wrath. A prayer meeting was held with this intent in the evening, and the following Sabbath was proposed as a day of prayer and humiliation before God.

24 November. Visited the people in their houses. From this day's experience we are constrained to praise God, who is doing great things for us. A spirit of prayer is more general among the people than I could have expected. Of many who we supposed never had a serious thought about their souls we were constrained to say, Behold they pray!

14 January 1832, Sunday. In the evening 29 wagons arrived, all loaded with people who came to attend the services of religion. Mr Jenkins of Bootschap, being here, addressed a crowded congregation.[9]

18 January. Vaccinated 26 persons. The school increased to 90 children. Service in the evening—102 attended.

22 January, Sunday. The number of candidates exceeding 30, it was thought necessary to divide them into two classes, and to converse with one class on Sabbath between services and with the other class on Thursday afternoons.

25 January. Service in the evening. 100 attended. At the conclusion of the service spake with the candidates. The Lord verily blessed us; every heart appeared to feel and every eye did weep.

29 January, Sunday. This day being appointed as a day of thanksgiving to Almighty God for having mercifully delivered us from that dreadful disease the smallpox, Mr Jenkins preached to 400 persons. After the service many of the people prayed.[10] I preached in the afternoon and evening.

5 February, Sunday. Two elders and two deacons were chosen by the unanimous voice of the members. Our church discipline is as follows. If a member conduct himself unbecomingly, he is reprimanded; if this proceeding have no effect, two other members endeavour to convince him of his error. If their endeavours fail, the subject is brought before the missionary, elders and deacons, and their conclusion is laid before the whole church. The votes of the members decide the questions brought forward.

12 February, Sunday. Prayer meeting in the morning as usual. 250 attended. 300 attended the other services of religion. This has been a day of apparent spiritual awakening to some. The

6. Source: CWMA 170 (Report, 1831).
7. A note to the version of the journal published in the *Evangelical Magazine* IX (Sept. 1833) added to this: "Mr Kolbe afterwards speaks of his weariness of body in the spiritually delightful duties of the day, and closes by remarking, in reference to the people among whom it is his privilege to labour, 'It is now 10 o'clock, yet we still hear prayers and hymns of praise ascending to God and our Saviour Jesus Christ. May the Lord bless His own work!'".
8. Gideon Joubert, field cornet of New Hantam in the Colesberg district.
9. Thomas Jenkins of the Wesleyan mission station Buchuaap (Boetsap) beyond the Vaal.
10. That is, presumably, prayed extempore.

conversation with the members and candidates was edifying and encouraging. Four English ladies and two Dutch Colonists attended the service.

15 February. Some Bushmen having stolen two heifers belonging to our people, two parties went out last night in quest of the thieves. This morning many Bushmen were brought to the station. The delinquents were discovered and whipped, and the other Bushmen were sent away with presents of meat &c. This is another proof that Bushmen may be brought to punishment for their depredatory acts, and that in many cases (as in this) there is no need of discharging a gun, much less of shooting them.

20 February. 110 children attended the school.

27 February. Employed between school hours in visiting the houses. The Word of God is proving a savour of life unto many.

1 April, Sunday. In the morning 200 persons attended the prayer meeting. Our new church being so far ready, we were able to hold service in it today. This building has been erected entirely by the inhabitants of the district of Philippolis. The Society[11] assisted with 200 rixdollars (£15) and some nails, hinges, screws, &c. It will contain 500 persons. The walls are of stone, two feet and a half thick and 12 feet high. Today the church was filled and the aisles crowded, and 100 were obliged to remain in the street. Four children were baptised; two members also were admitted by baptism to church fellowship. In the evening the whole congregation was melted into tears during the administration of the sacrament.

2 April. 335 children in the school.

3 April. At the catechising of the children this afternoon many adults attended.

9 April. Rode to Dice [*sic*] Fountain (5 miles distant from this place).[12] All the scholars requested to go with me. I took as many as the wagon could contain. Such affection is very pleasing. On my return they (the children) sung many hymns, which quite excited my feelings. At 5 o'clock met the members of the church.

15 April, Sunday. In the evening a Griqua came desiring to speak to me. He stated that for some time past he had had great prejudices against me and my preaching, that he was sorry for it and begged my forgiveness. I said that I had always been praying for him, and freely forgave him all the evil thoughts which he had harboured against me. I advised him to refrain from commandoes,[13] and to seek Christ as his Saviour.

1 May. This afternoon a little girl 8 years old was greatly affected in school whilst repeating the fourth commandment. I asked her the cause of her grief; she replied, I feel that I have sinned, and that I do not turn with my whole heart to Jesus. She prayed; she knew Jesus would accept so great a sinner as she was, and she desired to seek Him with her whole heart.—Another female was also much affected during the catechetical instructions.

6 May, Sunday. We trust that the Spirit taught us to pray, for the blessing of the Lord was evidently with us during the prayer meeting. During the morning service the congregation was much affected. One person left the chapel, being overcome by his feelings. I greatly rejoiced at the conclusion of the service to see any persons going to the hills and ravines to pour out their supplications before God. O Lord —notwithstanding my unworthiness— O Lord, send us now prosperity! Our Chief, though no member of the church, is exemplary in his conduct, and attends the services.

8 May. After dinner rode to a horde of Corannas who were afflicted with the smallpox. Found two persons attacked with this disease. Exhorted them to believe on Jesus and to prepare for eternity. One of these persons appeared to enjoy the comforts of religion.

11. The LMS.
12. Probably Driefontein, a farm 8km to the northwest of Philippolis which Kolbe had bought from his predecessor Melvill.
13. That is, presumably, from going out on raiding expeditions.

23 May. Having preached various sermons against drunkenness, calling upon the Chief and his Council from love to their country, to their people and to their own souls to do all in their power to prevent the bad practice which the Colonists have of bringing brandy into this country, I rejoice to hear that the Chief has prohibited the sale of spirits at the station.

26 May. A Griqua who came from Graham's Town with a load of goods to this station stopped at Okkert Schalkwyk's (a Colonist residing near this station), where he had so much brandy given him to drink by the Boor that he as found dead in his bed the next morning.[14]

2 June. Today we were informed that a person had shot a Griqua in a fit of drunkenness. The ball had entered his hip, but his life was not despaired of.

9 July. Commenced the quarterly visitation of the people at their houses. At the first house we called we found that all the inmates worshipped God. Three females who have been for some time under religious instruction were admitted as candidates. The next family we visited appeared to be careless, formal, without the true knowledge which is in Christ Jesus. In another family we spoke with an elderly female who had been for some time under conviction of her sins. In the last house we entered the father of the family was a man of much religious knowledge; had formerly been a member of the Church, but appears now to be a hardened, impenitent sinner.

14 July. How anxiously should a missionary endeavour to gain the hearts of the people among whom he labours, and by his own example evince that religion consists not in words, but in deeds. This week the Lord has greatly blessed us. Seven persons have been admitted as candidates, and many are under religious impressions.

15 July, Sunday. 400 persons attended the services of religion, Mr Peel, a Wesleyan, who is compelled to remain a few months here, requested to be considered a member of our church during his stay.[15] He observed "that he verily found God was at this place among His children".

21 July. The Veld Cornet Joubert (the nearest Veld Cornet to this boundary)[16] and two other farmers arrived here this afternoon for the purpose of obtaining medical advice, and also to attend the religious services of this station.

22 July, Sunday. 400 persons attended the services of religion, among whom were four Dutch Colonists, four English traders and an English female.[17]

5 August, Sunday. Our chapel was filled, yea, literally crammed. 500 persons attended the various services of religion, among whom were a Dutch Colonist, three English traders, Captain Waterboer and his Council from Griqua Town, and a few persons from Bootschap.[18] Two adults and one infant were baptised.

6 August. 200 persons attended the missionary prayer meeting.

12 August, Sunday. 400 persons attended the services of religion, among whom were 80 Bechuanas.

1 September. Service as usual. 300 attended. After service met the members for prayer and self-examination preparatory to the sacrament.[19]

2 September, Sunday. 500 persons attended the different services of religion.

3 September. A meeting was called for the purpose of commencing a temperance society. Several persons addressed the meeting, and 83 signed as members. Joseph de Bruin (a member

14. Ockert van Schalkwyk was one of the earliest white Colonists to settle in Griqua territory. He was a man of ungovernable temper, and caused much trouble to the Griqua and Colonial authorities.
15. Peel has not been further identified.
16. See n8 above.
17. As distinct from a "lady".
18. The Wesleyan mission Buchuaap (Boetsap) beyond the Vaal.
19. i.e. Communion.

of the church) promised that the use of spirits should be entirely discontinued, even for medicinal purposes, for he observed that under the name of using spirits as medicine drunkenness would secretly be indulged in. This proposition was unanimously agreed to, with an amendment. A memorial was also presented to the Chief and Council, signed by all the members, requesting him to issue an order that all spirits brought from the Colony for the purpose of trafficking in this district should be considered as contraband and forfeited goods.[20]

One constant grievance on the part of Kolbe, as on that of his predecessor Melvill, was the scattered condition of the people, and in October 1835, in submitting one of his habitually enthusiastic reports on the progress of the station to the Directors in London, he added the characteristic refrain:

It is, however, much to be regretted that the roving disposition so universal among the Colonial Farmers exerts its influence upon our people. The great extent of territory in this district induces many to leave their farms, on which they could subsist with some labour, in search of stronger springs, though at a great distance from the station, where less labour is required and game more abundant. Could they be induced to erect substantial houses upon their farms, their roving inclination would in some measure be checked, but at present the semi-Europeans who about four years ago located themselves near this station have dispersed themselves to other parts of the country or settled at places far distant from the station, and thus deprived themselves of the means of grace and education for their children. Could we concentrate our population, much more success would attend our missionary labours. The dispersed state of the people prevents us getting that assistance which otherwise would be expected in the erecting of publick buildings &c.[21] It is our constant endeavour to pourtray in the plainest manner the advantages of permanent settlement and industrious habits, as tending to the spiritual and temporal benefit of their posterity, but this is no easy task, for present gain induces them to forget or neglect future beneficial good. Perseverance is our only rule, prayer and faith alone our consolations.[22]

In spite of these complaints, which would remain perennial on the part of the missionaries at Philippolis, a great deal was in fact being done on the various outposts in the district by local evangelists and teachers, even though their endeavours may not have enjoyed the blessing of the missionaries themselves. An illustration of this is provided in the description by the German missionary Reinhold Gregorowski of a journey from Philippolis to the Riet River in the winter of 1835, which at the same time provides a glimpse of two former employees of the LMS, Piet Sabba and Jan Goeyman.

We arrived at Saba's place about half past seven in the evening, and found a large Griqua kraal. Many of the people had gathered together in a hut in which Saba was at that minute holding evening service. He read a chapter from the Bible and accompanied the text with a few explanations. After the prayer, "*Hy, die den Heiland nog niet heeft,/ Is dood en zonder God*" &c. was sung. Saba told us that all the people gathered together in this hut were Griquas, and how he had formerly lived in Griquatown and received instruction from the missionary Anderson. Goemann, an-

20. Cf. Backhouse, as quoted in Schreiner, p.37; also ibid, p.41.—Source of quotation: CWMA Journals 1596.
21. As an example of the amount of editing missionary documents underwent before appearing in print, it may be mentioned that when this last sentence in Kolbe's letter eventually saw the light, it read: "The dispersion of the people excludes us from getting that assistance in the erecting of publick buildings &c which otherwise might be expected".—It must be added, however, that Kolbe's letters seem to have received particularly close attention from the editors of the LMS's publications in London.
22. Source: CWMA 202 (20.10.1835).

other Griqua, who had moved away from them a few days before, had conducted the morning service hitherto, and he himself the evening service. Goemann had also taught reading, but as he had only had a single school book, and had taken it with him, the instruction could not be continued.[23]

During Kolbe's period of office at Philippolis the Transgariep experienced great changes. In 1830 the village of Colesberg was established across the Orange as the nearest Colonial settlement and seat of British authority, with a magistrate and civil commissioner and a Dutch church. Philippolis was therefore no longer an outpost of Christianity and western civilization on the outer fringes of Colonial society.

Secondly, the Paris Missionary Society began its work among the Basotho of Moshweshwe in the Caledon River valley in 1833, and at the same time one of their missionaries also settled at Bushman School, which was transferred to them by Dr Philip after the mission to the Bushmen had been abandoned by the LMS. They renamed the station Bethulie, and established there a station for the refugee Tlhaping of Chief Lephoi who had been hitherto living in the Philippolis district under the protection of the Griquas. In 1834 again the Berlin Missionary Society founded the station of Bethanie near the Riet River, in Griqua territory, for the Right Hand Korana ("Regshande") of Goliat Yzerbek. For all these missionaries Philippolis was a centre from which they might obtain assistance or advice when required, and where they halted on their way to and from the Colony. Many travellers also began to journey through the area, most notably the scientific expedition under Andrew Smith in the summer of 1834–35.

During this period descriptions of the station also became more frequent. The following account is by August Gebel of the Berlin Missionary Society, describing the first sight of the village when he and his colleagues arrived there with the expedition of Andrew Smith.

On Thursday morning, 28 August [1834], we reached Philippolis, the station of the missionary Kolbe, the furthest point in this direction which is entirely inhabited by Basters and where Dutch is spoken. (...) Apart from the church we counted 13 houses, but partly uncompleted, partly dilapidated. The fully independent Captain, Adam Kok, who can call up 600 fighting men, is a rich man and well disposed towards all missionaries; however, his right hand and his brain is his son-in-law, Henrik Henrik,[24] a warrior famous and to some extent also feared throughout the Colony, who some time ago even fought against Moselekazzi.[25]

Kolbe is described by Gebel on the same occasion as "a lively, powerful man of about 32–34 years, the son of a German by birth, although he has never been to Germany, but he understands German books quite well".[26]

The French missionary Eugéne Casalis again, writing in October 1833, gave the following description of the village and mission station.

At this period all the Basters and the Griquas who make up Mr Kolbe's flock had returned from a hunting expedition, and I was able to form a better judgment of Philippolis from the point of view of missionary activity.[27] A traveller who spends only two or three days on this station would run the risk of judging it unfavourably, for most of the natives live at some distance from the establishment. But when one sees on Saturday the wagons laden

23. Source: BMB (1835), p.29 (translated from the German).
24. Hendrik Hendrickze.
25. Hendrickze had participated in a disastrous expedition against the amaNdebele of Mzilikazi which had taken place in the winter of 1831 under the leadership of Barend Barends, Baster Kaptyn of Boetsap,— Source of quotation: BMB (1835), p.29 (translated from the German).
26. Source: BMB (1835), p.40 (translated from the German).
27. i.e., in contrast to his earlier visit in May of the same year, when the French missionaries were on their way to the Basotho.

with men, women and children arriving for the service, one can only bless the Lord and admire the enlightened zeal of the London Missionary Society. Already many people have been brought to a true and practical knowledge of Christianity.

After the public service on Sunday the faithful gather to tell one another of their experiences and exercise the right of fraternal reprimand. I had the joy of assisting at the reception of two new members. What a moving scene! How beautiful it was to see the neophytes standing near the pulpit, listening with emotion to the solemn exhortations of their pastor and, receiving a short while afterwards the pledges of their Saviour's love![28]

Gebel also described a church service he attended on the station.

On Sunday, 30 August [1834] we heard Kolbe preach on [II?] Cor. 5:1–10 in his church, which can hold more than 300 people. The singing of the heavy English melodies was quite surprisingly true. The London Society has on each of its stations introduced its own little hymnal with Dutch translations of English hymns, such as the well-known "Remember me", the favourite hymn of Henry Martin.[29] The Hottentot tribes are in general able to sing well, much more so than the Kaffirs.

On Sunday, 31 August Kraut preached;[30] I had to remain at the wagons to allow the others to go to church. At noon I conducted an English service in the camp;[31] in the afternoon I heard the true Hottentot language for the first time, when Kolbe preached on the text "One thing is needful" in Dutch, while the abovementioned Henrik translated it for the Korannas who were present.[32] After this service we remained behind in the church for an hour with the actual members of the congregation and the [baptismal] candidates while Kolbe spoke to them singly about the state of their souls and their experiences during the past week. He has approximately 30 full members of the church, i.e. communicants, and celebrates the Sacrament every two months.[33]

Judged by externals, Kolbe's ministry at Philippolis would seem to have been a success. While the summaries of mission affairs published in the annual reports of the LMS may have been highly selective, they were not deliberately incorrect, and their statistics are on the whole probably to be trusted even after having been wrenched from their proper context in the accounts submitted by the missionaries.

"We are happy to observe," the official report for 1833, published in 1834, remarked on Philippolis in surveying the events of the previous year, "that the good work is steadily advancing at this station; and though many fears have been excited by external causes, yet the Lord has graciously preserved the people from the reckless violence of the ungodly."[34]

During the visit of the French missionaries to Philippolis in 1833, Kolbe had on 26 May had been ordained minister by them.[35] "This has been to me a most solemn day," he noted in his journal on that date,

28. i.e., partaking of Communion.—Source of quotation: JME (1834), pp.136–7 (translated from the French).
29. Henry Martyn, a well-known English missionary of the time, who had died in the East in 1812.
30. His companion, G.A. Kraut. The German party consisted of three missionaries.
31. That of Smith's expedition.
32. Another reference to Hendrik Hendrickze.
33. Source: BMB (1835), pp.38–9 (translated from the German).
34. Report (1834), p.95.
35. The missionaries in the party were Prosper Lemue, J.P. Pellissier, Thomas Arbousset, Eugéne Casalis and Constant Gossellin (all mentioned in the account quoted below); the first named were both newly married, and accompanied by their wives, Eléonore Lemue and Martha Pellissier. The Lemues were on their way to Mothito (Bothitong) in the interior, while the Pellissiers remained at Philippolis provisionally before moving to Bushman Station and the three unmarried men undertook the mission to the Basotho.

the day on which I have been publicly ordained as a minister of the Gospel. Br. Le Mue preached the sermon from the words of Christ to Nicodemus, the wind bloweth &c., this being the day held by many Christians in commemoration of the outpouring of the Holy Spirit upon the apostles.[36] At the conclusion of the sermon I addressed the people at Br. Le Mue's request, exhorting them to pray for what has been wrought among them, and to pray for the outpouring of the Spirit. Br. Le Mue spoke to the congregation assembled on the subject of ordination, asked the questions and offered up the ordination prayer. Messrs Pellisier and Arbusset joined him during the imposition of hands. When the right hand of fellowship and the kiss of charity was given, and after I had made another short address to the people, we were dismissed with the Lord's blessing.—In the afternoon Br. Pellisier preached. We concluded to partake of the Lord's Supper in the evening ere we departed from each other. Br. Casalis and Gosselin were much to our sorrow detained at the river, for we trust that the Lord revealed Himself to us, and that we all felt the powerful influence of the Holy Spirit. May the Lord grant us grace to be faithful servants in His vineyard.[37]

In 1835 the published annual report for Philippolis, covering the year 1834, read as follows:

The people of this station amount to 357 male and 358 female adults and 900 children; total, 1615 persons.

The work of the Lord has continued to prosper, and those who have professed Christ, walk according to the Gospel. The gradual progress of Christianity in this part of Southern Africa has been such that the Missionary observes: "We can now say, we live in a Christian country, and Christianity is established among us."

The Sabbath Day congregations are usually from 250 to 500, and those on the weekdays are from 60 to 200. The church, to which have been added 6 members during the year, now consists of 37 members. There are 6 candidates for communion. Six adults and 15 children have been baptized, and the number of adults [who are] candidates for baptism is 8. Thirteen couples have been united by legal marriage.

The day school contains 50 children. Mr Kolbe has also established an infant school.

Of religious tracts 400 have been distributed.

The Temperance Society.—The members have increased from 87 to 203. The opponents of this society when it first commenced have now become its staunch advocates. Drunkenness, which was lately a pest in the land, has now ceased.

At the last Anniversary of the Philippolis Auxiliary Missionary Society, 91 persons signed their names as annual subscribers to the amount of 270 rix-dollars, or £20 5s.

It is gratifying to learn that the country round Philippolis had been preserved from the devastations of locusts, and that in December last [1834] (the date of the latest tidings), the Missionary states: "Our people are now reaping an abundant harvest."

From the commencement of this station in 1831,[38] 118 converts to Christianity have been baptized.[39]

The official report for the year 1835, published early in 1836, though briefer, was equally sanguine.

Religion, civilization and good order have made some advance at this station, and the blessing of peace has attended it. Several have been added to the church, which at the end of the year

---

36. The references are respectively to John 3:8 ("The wind bloweth where it listeth, and thou hearest the sound thereof, but canst not tell whence it cometh"); and Acts 2.
37. Source: CWMA Journals 1596–1597.
38. I.e., the commencement of Kolbe's work here.
39. Source: Report (1835), pp.94–95.

consisted of 32 members walking steadily in their profession. One has died in the faith; four have gone to other stations; one has been admitted to full communion; and two adults and 51 children have been baptized. Candidates for baptism, nine; for communion, four.

The Sabbath services are three—morning, afternoon and evening; and there are also services and prayer meetings during the week, all of which are well attended. The attendance on the Sabbath is from 200 to 400; on weekdays from 80 to 200.

Schools.—Average attendance in day schools, 42; infant schools, 45. The children have made very commendable progress. A new school is erecting, the present building being neither sufficiently large nor convenient. Five bibles, four Testaments and 200 tracts have been distributed within the year.

Adam Kok, the Chief of Philippolis, died on his return from Cape Town last year. The object of his visit to the latter place was to have entered into a treaty with the government, as the Chief Waterboer had done, but unhappily, after waiting there some months, he was obliged to depart without seeing the Governor, whose presence had been required on the frontier. No written treaty has been yet entered into with this people.[40]

By the time this account was made public, however, Kolbe had become involved in a scandal which was to cause his departure from Philippolis before the end of the year. Because of the light it throws on the disunity and tensions in missionary circles as well as on the affairs of the mission and the Captaincy at Philippolis, this needs to be described in some detail, trivial though the events may seem in themselves.

During 1836, when Dr Philip was once again absent on a protracted visit to England and J.J. Freeman was acting in his place, reports reached Cape Town that Kolbe had been accused of adul-

tery with the wife of one of the members of his congregation, the Baster Andries Wiese.[41]

It was seemingly on account of these allegations that Theophilus Atkinson, a young missionary working at Bethelsdorp, was despatched by Freeman to Philippolis, where he arrived in August 1836, and shortly afterwards a formal investigation of the charges against Kolbe appears to have been conducted by the missionaries of the neighbouring French stations, who found him innocent. Atkinson, however, was soon drawn into the marital problems of the Kolbes as a confidant of Margaret Kolbe, and seems to have had second thoughts on the subject, which resulted in his undertaking something very much resembling a witch hunt against his colleague.

The first of the sequence of letters providing information on subsequent developments was written by Kolbe on 9 January 1837 to the Secretary of the LMS in London.

Reverend and dear Sir, —Your communication of 27 May /36 I duly received, and feel very thankful for your advice therein contained. I should gladly have followed your directions in everything at Philippolis, but it is now my painful duty to transmit to you such intelligence as must excite your intense sorrow, as it deeply grieves my own soul.

40. Adam Kok II had gone to Cape Town with the intention of entering into a treaty with the British authorities similar to that concluded by Andries Waterboer, the Kaptyn at Griquatown, in 1834. The Governor being absent in the Eastern Province on account of the Sixth Frontier War, however, and his own health deteriorating, he had decided to return to Philippolis, and died on the Berg River on 12 September 1835.—Source of quotation: Report (1836), p.98.
41. Wiese had in 1831 received permission from the Landdrost of Graaff-Reinet to remove to Griquatown "under the Chief Adam Kok" [sic]; CA, 1/GR 10/4 (1.8.1831). He is mentioned by Andrew Smith as *wykmeester* at Philippolis in 1834, and also seems to have worked as a blacksmith. In later years he is reported as living between Norval's Pont and Philippolis.

You will permit me to advert to past events, and suffer me to state that after being employed five years as a missionary at Graaff Reinet without ever having incurred the least blame upon my character, I joined your honoured Society during the Revd Mr Miles' superintendence, and laboured three years with Mr James Clark among the Bushmen, whose opinion as to my character, as his late letters testify, is very pleasing. I have now been employed nearly seven years at Philippolis. My labors have been greatly blessed. I have been the instrument in the hands of God —to Him alone be all the glory!—of raising a large congregation forming a Christian church of more than 40 members, assisted building with my own hands, and much of my own expence, a large school, infant school, &c., and always had, down to the last time I preached, a large and numerous congregation.

Your are also partly informed of the many trials I have had to encounter in the work of the Lord, how the Griquas once robbed me of cattle, and used every endeavour to injure me, so that Dr Philip in one of his letters to me at that time says that they wished to compel me to leave Philippolis. However, with the help of the Almighty I proceeded in my work, and my labors were repaid by the tender love of the people of God towards me, and their affectionate sympathy to me in all my trials.[42] My enemies continued their accusations against me, they complained that I had too much attachment to a party, and I certainly did love those that loved the Word of God more than those that despised it. Were I to communicate all the injuries attempted to be done to me by Hendrik Hendriks, who has been my greatest enemy and had the most influence in the country, although guilty of many enormous crimes, I should quite tire your patience, and intrude on your precious time. I could convince you how often he was publickly proved to be a calumniator and slanderer of my character. I shall, however, advert to two circumstances only.

On August 17, 1832 this person wrote to me a threatening letter informing me that if I did not alter my manner of preaching and making allusions to the affair of Masselikatse, I could fear the consequences.[43] I continued fearlessly to preach the Gospel, but I soon found he had determined to use every effort to ruin me. Many false reports he raised and circulated.

In 1835, when he returned with the Chief from a visit to Graaff Reinet, they brought a large quantity of brandy, and intoxicated nearly all the people, then he ex[c]ited the Chief to expel me with force from the country, as appeared afterwards, on the ground of my having taught the people too much to know their own rights and privileges, and they had become too knowing, as the Chief expressed it, to be governed by him while I remained among them. I was summoned before the Council, a party of unlawful Councillors selected on purpose. I replied to about eight false accusations this H.H. brought against me, and he joined finally with the Chief and Council in declaring me in all things innocent.

Hendrik Hendrik[s] came into my own house in an intoxicated state, cursed, swore and abused me in a scandalous manner in the presence of my wife and children, and threatened me with personal danger if I dared to hold service on the coming Sabbath. I should not have cared for his threats, but the elders and deacons advised, in consideration of the intoxicated state of the people, it would be better to refrain from performing the Sabbath duties. After this transaction the Chief testified publicly to the French brethren that he knew nothing against me.

It was this Hendriks that also circulated the report about Mrs E. Wiese and myself. The Revd Mr Freeman, I trust, has laid

42. A reference to the local Baster congregation or "Old Inhabitants", as opposed to the Griquas on the station.
43. This was the raid on the amaNdebele which had taken place the year before; see n25 above.

before you the report of the whole proceedings, and how my enemies could prove nothing against me, as the documents of the French missionaries evince. I felt certainly, Reverend Sir, much hurt at the appointment of Mr Atkinson to my station before an investigation had taken place, and it grieved me to perceive the ready belief which Dr Philip had paid to the report. When I was at the Kat River with the late Chief just before the Caffre War, the Doctor informed me that he had heard reports concerning me.[44] He proposed my removal from Philippolis, to which proposal I readily acceded, but Mr Monro of Grahamstown was not willing to remove his sphere of labor, and the Doctor wished to have me at Grahamstown.[45] Had Dr Philip removed me then, or acceeded to my own proposal for removal when I perceived the drift of my adversaries, much grief and sorrow had been prevented. It is true that in 1836, when my character had been traduced, the Doctor strongly urged my removal, but I refused before an investigation had been made as to the report against me. I told the Doctor I could not leave with such a stigma on my character, and it would not be just to admit an investigation during my absence. The Revd Mr Freeman advised me how to act further, and I did accordingly. This gentleman also wrote to me to proceed in my labors.

I had retired from the station after the investigation of the French brethren, but at the solicitation of Mr Atkinson I returned to Philippolis, and for some months we co-operated harmoniously together, but an unfortunate occurrence, to which I shall just now reluctantly allude, discovered that Mr Atkinson, although professing and acting as a brother in the work of the Lord with me, had private conference with Mrs Kolbe to my injury, without ever speaking to me on the subject. And be it observed that on 12 August [1836] Mr A. arrived here, on the 14 September [he] left for a visit to the French brethren and returned October 15 to Philippolis, and on Thursday the 19th the following occurrence took place. I premise these observations that you may see, Reverend Sir, that Mr Atkinson had been prejudiced by others against me, and had not time to judge from personal observation.

On the 19 October in the evening I returned with my wagon from the Orange River, to which place I had accompanied Capt. Sutton,[46] and brought a packet of letters for Mr Atkinson. My wagon halted at Mr A.['s] house, and my children, as it was a moonlight night, came all running to the wagon to meet me. I went to Mr Atkinson's door, but found he was asleep. I returned, and called Andries Wiese, who had driven my wagon, out of his house to drive the wagon home. I went into the street, while he remained to get some tobacco, and stood there waiting by the front oxen till he came. Here I unexpectedly met Mrs Kolbe with one of the young children in her arms, and with heartfelt pain I must say she was exasperated to a high degree. I explained to her my conduct, but passion was triumphant. I advised her to come home, and took her by the hand, endeavouring to soothe her feelings till we could privately converse together. She, however, seated herself upon the ground and called repeatedly as loud as possible, "Mr Atkinson!" I felt irritated, and said to my eldest daughter, "Come home with your mother." I pulled my hand from Mrs K.'s grasp, and in the act the back of my hand came in contact with her cheek. Mrs Wiese came out of her house, and Mrs K. and she had some words together. I expected that Mrs K. would come home, but when I enquired, I understood that she had gone to Mr A.'s house, where she remained till the next day in the afternoon, though I had early in the morning demanded Mr A. to send Mrs Kolbe to me.

The Friday morning Mr A. came to me with a Mr Davidson,

---

44. This visit had taken place at the end of 1834.
45. John Monro was working among the Khoikhoi at Grahamstown.
46. William Sutton, who was in 1845 to be appointed the first British Resident in the Transgariep.

one of the members of the Church,⁴⁷ and began to accuse me of cruel treatment to Mrs Kolbe, and with many threats insisted on another investigation by Mr Wright of Griquatown and himself. I objected, and said rather than be harassed in such a manner I would resign the duties of the station into his hands and appeal to the Directors. I expressed my surprise at Mr A.'s conduct—not a word of private conversation or brotherly advice to me [or?] profession of love to me, and yet to act in such a manner is what I never could have expected from a Christian brother, but from a secret enemy. In no other light I look upon Mr A.'s conduct than as one who was disappointed in my innocence, and wished to supplant me.

In his conversation Mr A. accused me of having frequently beaten Mrs Kolbe. Now, Reverend Sir, I readily appeal to the Searcher of Hearts and to the day of final retribution that this is totally false. I did not beat Mrs K. on the evening Mr A. alluded to. I have been kind and affectionate to my wife at all times, and everybody who knows me must confess if they will testify the truth that my character has never been tarnished even by my enemies with cruelty or harshness. Mr Atkinson says Mrs K. fainted away the evening alluded to; this was not in my presence, but I know Mrs K. is subject to fainting fits, which might have been brought on by her ex[c]ited feelings. I defied Mr A. to show the least black or red mark on Mrs K.'s body as a proof of his false accusation, and which he could not do.

Mr A. also confessed that he had had conversation with members of the Church who he refused to name, and that they were dissatisfied with the proceedings of the French brethren as to their investigation. I conceived it very unseemly after Mr Atkinson had signed the document of the French missionaries to join with the members in private condemnation of their actions. Mr A. also said he had read part of a letter shown him by Mrs Kolbe, addressed to me by Mrs Wiese, which induced him to have suspicions against me. This letter was not produced, and I deny ever having received a letter of the contents alluded to by Mr A. By whom it may have been written, I know not, but I do not believe the said person wrote it, and I wish the accuser to produce his proofs.

Mr A. further accuses me of having acted imprudently in frequenting more than before the house of Wiese, and, finally, of commencing a shop in that house. Now I must inform you that I had long before this occurrence purchased the house alluded to, with a view to his (Wiese) leaving the station, and intending that my eldest son, whom I daily expected from school, commence a small store there. As I have a family of ten children,[48] and am only 33 years of age, it will probably increase, and I thought I should not act improper in this respect. I beg here just to mention that I have not drawn my full salary since engaged in the service of your Society, and thought to have been enabled by this means to have needed less, and prevented the people from being imposed upon by unprincipled traders. I confess that for two weeks I did more frequently visit the house, which I had purchased, of Wiese, but it was at the request of Capt. C. Kok of Campbell,[49] who was then on a visit with his wife and family, and who wished to consult me on various subjects. He was also taken very ill, and I had many days to attend to him. On the grounds already alluded to, I had purchased goods for my son. The visit and sickness of Kok prevented Wiese removing as soon as I could have wished, and my son was also detained on his way. As I was obliged to remit my payments, I was obligated

47. Probably Alexander Davidson, who is known to have traded beyond the Orange River and was a deacon of the church at Philippolis. However, a blacksmith called Davidson is also mentioned at Philippolis, and this may have been Adam Davidson: Alexander and Adam, who were possibly brothers, both came to the Cape in 1817.
48. While Kolbe must be presumed to have known the number of his own children, according to the genealogies he and his wife had eight children at this time, a ninth having died in infancy.
49. Cornelius Kok II, brother of the late Adam Kok II.

myself to dispose of the goods I had purchased, and I did not wish to keep the articles of traffick in the mission house, which was fully occupied by my family.

Davidson, Mr Atkinson's witness, also made a false charge against me, stating that in the memorial Mr Freeman has, I trust, kindly laid before you, names were inserted without knowledge of the subscribers. On investigation Davidson could not provide a single proof to substantiate his assertion, and was fully proved to be a false accuser.

The following note I addressed October 21 to Mr Atkinson. "Reverend Sir, I have authority in the name of Mrs Kolbe to inform you that I never was guilty of beating Mrs K. at any time. I intend further to proceed as usual in my duties as missionary of Philippolis, subject to the interference of no person save the Directors of the Society." Mr Freeman had left,[50] and we had no agent. Mr A. in reply expressed his surprise at the contents, and stated, "I was just coming up to enquire what was your intention respecting the services in the church, but it is now unnecessary; as you decline any further interference in your labors, I shall certainly not attempt any, and consequently decline taking any further part in the services of the station."

Knowing it to be the wish of the church and of the Chief and Council that Mr A. and I should co-operate together, and that he mistook my meaning, I wrote in reply to this effect: "You have misunderstood the word 'interference'. I meant that any complaints respecting my proceedings can only be referred to the Directors. Believe me, Reverend Sir, I will most affectionately unite with you in the religious services of the station, burying anything disagreeable that may have occurred in oblivion, and cordially proceed according to an arrangement which we may think proper to make, should you please to give me your call for this purpose." I was informed in reply "that although I might have put a different construction upon your words from what you have intended, my determination remains the same. I cannot under present circumstances unite with you in the religious services of the station." Consequently I conducted all the services the following Sabbath alone, and all the people of the village and others attended.

After mature deliberation, knowing that Mr A. would write unfavourable reports concerning me, that the feelings of Dr Philip were not as formerly towards me owing to the calumniations of my foes, and that it was the Doctor's wish that I should leave Philippolis, as he stated in his last letter to me, whether I was found innocent or guilty of the accusations against me, I conceived it better again to retire to a small farm I had purchased of Mr Melvill,[51] and to wait the decision of the Directors. I therefore wrote to Mr Atkinson October 24 that I resigned for the present the duties of the station into his hands, which he readily accepted.

It grieves me to think that although I have in no wise interfered with Mr A.'s labors since this period, but attended his preaching, he has admitted all the members of the Church which were excommunicated or put under censure by the whole Church during the time I officiated as minister, without even privately consulting with me, although I told Mr Atkinson that I was willing to give him any information that he might require, and to lay the church books before him. Some of the people have abused the church authorities, lived in publick animosity, and are all re-admitted without any reconciliation to partake of the holy sacraments. If such things are tolerated, all that the excised members of the churches have to do at our stations is to desire another missionary when one who acts according to conscience and duty exercises church discipline towards them.

All the accusation that my enemies have been able to bring

---

50. Freeman had returned to England at the end of 1836.
51. Driefontein outside Philippolis.

amounts to this, that I have continued on intimate and friendly terms with the family of Wiese, but, Reverend Sir, I act in this instance from what I conceive to be just principles. Are our friends to suffer for and with us, to bear calumny and reproach for us, and are we to desert or hate them for their faithful friendship? The Word of God teaches me, "Thine own friend and thy father's friend forsake not."

Many of the people are preparing to leave Philippolis to settle beyond the territory of the present Chief.[52] They wish me to accompany them as their missionary. I am now waiting for the decision of the Directors. Should they disapprove in toto of my proceedings and approve of Mr Atkinson's conduct towards me, I have then, Reverend Sir, to return the Directors many thanks for all their kindness to me, to adore the goodness of that God who has suffered me, His unworthy servant, to remain so many years in the service of your Society, to depend upon His providence for the provision of my large family, and with all due deference to the Directors, I conceive the only course I can pursue is most respectfully to beg them to accept of my resignation, trusting that they will not admit of any ex parte statements without allowing me an opportunity of explaining and defending my conduct. I shall feel happy to give any further explanation that they may require.

Praying that the God of the Heathen may bless all your endeavours to propagate the Gospel of Salvation among the dying sons of men, I remain, Reverend Sir, your obedient and grateful servant, G.A. Kolbe.[53]

On 14 February 1837, Mrs Jane Philip, who after the departure of Freeman and in the absence of her husband was conducting the affairs of the Society, wrote from Cape Town to the Directors:

Philippolis has not been in a prosperous state this last year, but I hope that the removal of Mr Atkinson to that place will be the means of placing things on a better footing. It is very desirable that some decision should be early come to with respect to Mr Kolbe. Whatever doubts may exist of his guilt in the chief things laid to his charge, there can be no doubt respecting his great imprudence, and of his having wounded the feelings of his wife and caused much reproach to be cast on the mission cause. He has written requesting permission to begin another missionary station among the Corranas,[54] but I have answered him that under present circumstances I thought but he would not be justified in attempting anything of the kind till he heard from the Directors, as I was persuaded after they heard of the circumstances which occasioned his resignation at Philippolis (and an account of which had been sent to Dr Philip in England), the Directors would require a considerable time of trial even should he proffer repentance before he could be again employed as a missionary by the Society. To this letter I have as yet received no answer.[55]

In the meantime, Atkinson in turn had communicated directly with Philip in England, to whom he wrote as follows in January 1837.

It is useless to attempt to carry on the work with such a man as Kolbe at my elbow. I have long been convinced of his guilt as to the charge against him, but I now see that he is in every respect a wicked man.

He still talks as if he daily expected a letter from the Cape appointing him to another station, but I do not see how the So-

---

52. Abraham Kok, the son of Adam Kok II, during whose brief term of office there was much unrest and dissatisfaction in the Captaincy (see below).
53. Source: CWMA 212.
54. See Atkinson's remarks on this in the following letter.
55. Source: CWMA 203.

ciety can any longer employ him. He made an application lately to Jan Bloem to know if he would receive him as a missionary, but Jan told the messenger, "I am black enough myself, and what should I do with a still blacker?"[56] It is a great mercy he did not go to Bloem's people; it would set the whole country in an uproar to have such a man as he is among them. You will, however, be glad to hear that Bloem and his people are now under the care of the Griqua Town mission, and a school has been commenced at his place, and it is likely that he will enter into friendly arrangements with Waterboer. And if the union between the Griquas, and the treaty with the Colony, be completed, there will be a much better prospect of peace than at any time hitherto.[57]

But at this station everything is on the ground, church and state and education and morals and all. It will be an arduous work to bring things to a prosperous state, and I feel my inadequacy for this great task. But much may be done by vigorous exertion attended with the Divine blessing. There must, however, be another labourer. One cannot do what is necessary to be done.[58]

On 30 June 1837, Atkinson addressed himself as follows to the LMS in London.

I received a letter a few days ago from Mr Wright in which he mentioned the resolution contained in yours of December 31st [1836], and noticed particularly your request that he should come to Philippolis and engage with me in a fresh enquiry respecting Mr K.'s conduct. Circumstances, however, that have occurred since the last communications were sent you, induce us to think that we could not now with propriety enter upon another investigation. As Mr Wright will doubtless make known to you his views of the subject, I shall only state my own.

It does not appear that my letter to Dr Philip of October 26th had come under your notice previous to yours of 23rd March being sent.[59] I stated to Dr P. that in my interview with Mr Kolbe on 21st October I expressed to him my dissatisfaction with his line of conduct, and that for the honour of the Society I considered it necessary there should be another investigation, and on Mr K.'s inquiring who I meant should conduct it, I mentioned Mr Wright. He at once objected, as he considered Mr W. prejudiced against him, and "a man every way inferior" to him. I then asked him to name some other person, but he refused to admit to my further examination, and said that to save all further trouble, he would the next day send in his resignation to the Directors, and then we should have nothing more to do with his character. But instead of doing this, he signified to me in writing his determination to proceed on his duties as missionary at this station, subject to no interference but that of the Directors. In reply, I stated that I should decline taking any further part in the services of the station, and I immediately resolved on retiring from this place for a time.

On the 24th, however, Mr K. sent me his resignation as missionary at this station, and soon after retired to one of his farms in the neighbourhood. In January [1837] the Captain and his Council came to the resolution of sending Mr K. out of their district into the Colony, on the ground that they considered his residence here injurious to their interests. They allowed him some time to settle his affairs (as he was engaged in trade), and in the beginning of March he left this neighbourhood and went to Mr

56. Bloem, the son of a German father and a Kora mother, had been a notorious raider in his day. He was Chief of the Springbok Korana, for whom the German missionaries at Bethanie in 1845 established the station Pniel on the Vaal River (near the modern Barkly West).
57. A treaty between the Philippolis and Griquatown Captaincies was concluded on 25 February 1837, as a preliminary to a treaty between the former and the British authorities; see pp.98–99 below.
58. Source: CWMA 213.
59. Atkinson's letter to Philip had not been preserved.

Pellissier's station.[60] He soon afterwards sent for his family, and they have been residing there to the present time. Since then we have had no communication with each other, therefore I cannot say what Mr K.'s intentions are, or what the French missionaries have in contemplation concerning him. He is engaged at present in preaching for Mr Pellissier during his absence, and in the week is engaged in trade. Mr P. and his brethren still believe him innocent of the charge brought against him, and I have heard (though I cannot vouch for the truth of it) that they will receive him as a missionary under the French Society. Under these circumstances it does not appear necessary for Mr Wright and myself to institute a fresh inquiry.

It is needful to add that Mr W. was at Philippolis in January when the Council came to the above resolution. Indeed, they had invited him over to give his advice in reference to Mr K. And on account of the influence which Mr W. and I had with them in bringing them to this decision, Mr K. considered us both as his enemies. And consequently any inquiry conducted by us would be open to objection, and our report would be regarded as coming from prejudiced persons. I would therefore respectfully submit that if an inquiry still be considered desirable, Dr Philip be requested to conduct it on his return to this country, as his office as Superintendent would effectively preclude all reasonable objection. At the same time I may add, esteemed Fathers and Brethren, that should you still deem it expedient that Mr Wright and myself should enter upon the investigation, I shall consider it my duty, though a painful one, to comply with your request. In that case it would be well to have a third person engaged.[61]

Further developments had meanwhile been reported by Peter Wright of Griquatown to Jane Philip, writing directly from Philippolis on 1 February 1837.

My dear Mrs Philip,—I have little time to write till I get home, but I must send you a few lines from this. I arrived here on the 28th of December [1836], and owing to the state of things here I have been unavoidably detained nearly three weeks longer than expected. I intend to leave this tomorrow. Some of the Councillors and the Secretary accompany me to Griqua Town, being appointed to transact business with Waterboer.

On the 9th of January, at the request of the Lieutenant-Governor, Mr Atkinson and I met him at the River opposite to Colesberg.[62] I had much conversation with him there on Griqua matters. The Chief and Council of Philippolis met him at Colesberg two days previously, and I am glad that the opportunity afforded them ample time to converse with him on every subject connected with their interests. They are much pleased with the whole of Capt. Sto[c]kenstrom's proceedings in connection with their affairs, and it was finally concluded upon between the Governor and the Chief and Council that the latter would proceed to Griquatown to enter into treaty with Waterboer, and he would then at once treat with them.

Since their interview with the Governor the Chief and Councillors have been fully engaged in preparing the public mind for the proposed arrangements, in which they have been hitherto quite successful. Yesterday a general meeting was held, when a union with Waterboer and a treaty with the Colony were fully approved of by all. This is a great point gained; it is an important matter so far accomplished which I never expected to see, and I do hope the things will now meet with no further difficulties so far as it regards the ratification of the treaties. But the working of the new arrangement of things—in this we shall meet with serious difficulties, because with regard to both the Chief and a great

---

60. Bethulie.
61. Source: CWMA 213–214.
62. This was Andries Stockenstrom, who had meanwhile become Lieutenant Governor of the Eastern Province.

majority of the people (in this affair), they are raw, and it will require much that good Mr Atkinson does not possess to secure the establishment of a peaceable and prosperous state of things in the country. The success of the whole arrangement of things does not depend on the management of things at Griqua Town, but upon the management of matters here. Mr Atkinson is an excellent man and a good preacher. I am much pleased with him as a Christian and a preacher, and we must not blame him because he has not all the metal which the peculiarities of the situation demand.

Very considerable difficulties have been created here for the succeeding missionary by Kolbe's wicked conduct, and had he remained in the country, disappointment to the present missionary in his endeavours and much confusion and not unlikely bloodshed would have occurred. The numbers he has brought together and called a church are, with a very few exceptions, a mass of corruption, and the education of the youth of the station and of the district has been totally neglected. There are not half a dozen children to be found in the country which have been taught to read by him. The state of morals in the district is wretched to a degree, and at present he, Kolbe, seems to be at the head of the worst of the whoremongers and adulterers. His visits to Wiese's house are continued in spite of the remonstrances of all, and he has never been in the church during the five Sabbaths I have been here. The society he now keeps is the traders of the country, men of his own stamp; these rally round him. But I shall not go into detail in refference [*sic*] to his conduct. I shall just sum up by saying that I consider him a most wicked and dangerous man, and this I believe is the general opinion respecting him, both in these parts and in the Colony.

When the Lieutenant-Governor was at the River, the Griquas made him acquainted with the whole of his (Kolbe's) conduct, and that his presence in the country any longer was to be attended with numerous consequences, and they requested the

Governor to have him removed into the Colony. This the Governor refused to do, as he said he could not interfere on this side, but told them that as he (Kolbe) was injurious to their interests, they must send him into the Colony. In the first place they must request him to depart quietly, and if he refused, they must remove him by force. The Griquas have followed this advice. Kolbe refused in the first instance to go, but finding that they would remove him, he promised to depart, and he is to be clear off this week. He will make nearly Rds2000 of his fountains and erven. His livestock will bring him in a large sum.

When you express a hope that he may be restored to the ways of the Lord, you must not think that he ever was a religious man, for when he was first received as a missionary by our Society, we travelled together three or four days out of Graaff Reinet.[63] I had to leave leave his company on the road to save my own character, and it is now well known that no person of character either at Colesberg or in Graaff Reinet will allow him to enter their door. He has entered into business as a trader, and seems to have connections with the very worst of these characters, and he must be left to the choice he has made. It is impossible that he can be acknowledged in the Colony as connected with the Society. Whilst I have been here he has done his utmost to prevent a union of the two Griqua Chiefs and the treaty with the Colony, but with the *Zuid Afrikaan* newspaper in his hand and all the falsehoods he can fabricate against Dr Philip, Mr Fairbairn and myself, he has not only not succeeded,[64] but will in consequence leave this with the execrations of all except a few of the very

---

63. Nothing more is known of this journey. In a letter written from Griquatown early in 1828, however, Wright had contemplated a trip to Graaff-Reinet for the sake of his wife's health; CWMA 142 (25.2.1828).
64. John Fairbairn, the son-in-law and supporter of Philip, was the editor of the *Commercial Advertiser* in Cape Town, which thus in effect served as the mouthpiece of the missionary or "philanthropist" party, as opposed to the more critical *Zuid-Afrikaan*, edited by C.E. Boniface.

worst characters.⁶⁵

The note of unyielding vindictiveness which characterises Wright's references to his brother in Christ in this personal communication was kept up in the more formal letter written by him to the LMS from Griquatown on 19 July 1837.

Mr Kolbe's connection with the Griqua mission has been altogether from its commencement a most lamentable and disastrous matter, independent of the specific charges against his moral character. With regard to the investigation of those charges by the French missionaries, I must say it was entirely an ill-advised and badly-conducted thing, and owing to the consequent short triumph of Mr Kolbe and his party, and the violence and bitterness of factions where there is no head of government to control and regulate,⁶⁶ the results might have been for a long time very serious, both as it regards the tranquil[l]ity of the district and the missionary efforts of Mr K's successor. The truth of this remark Mr Atkinson soon found and felt severely when from his own observation he had learned Mr K.'s real character, had witnessed himself the circumstances which convinced him of Mr K. being guilty of those serious charges brought against him, and had his eyes opened to the strong undercurrent and feeling which was excited and directed by Mr K. against Mr A., and against all who were friends to truth and justice.

In these difficulties, and when the state of feeling was running very high between parties, I received letters in November last dated 21 and 24 October [1836] from Mr Atkinson, also from the Chief and Council of Philippolis and from other individuals, begging me to come over to see the state of things, and if possible to give them advice and render them assistance in their difficulties. The circumstance which had caused increased excitement at the time was the abuse of Mrs Kolbe in the street by Mr Kolbe and the family which had long had his frequent and untimely attentions, an account of which disgraceful circumstance I believe Mr Atkinson sent either to Dr Philip or to the Directors. The Chief and Council, and many of the decent people, were now determined to put an end to the confusion and disgrace. They called a meeting, and resolved to banish the infamous woman (who was the cause of all the disgrace) out of the district. But this resolution was not put into execution for fear of the possible consequence from the bad party. However, she with her family retired from the village to a farm of Mr K.'s behind the hills in the vicinity of the station. About the same time Mr K. resigned the duties of the station, left the village, and removed to another farm of his also behind some hills, only half an hour from the woman's dwelling, and his visits continued as usual. Owing to various important circumstances, I was not able to leave home till the 22nd of December [1836], and I arrived at Philippolis on the 29th, where I found Mr Atkinson and the affairs of the mission in great difficulties, owing to Mr K.'s ruinous effect and destructive influence against the mission. On my arrival I saw that with Kolbe and his party there was nothing to be done, and to allay feeling (which was the first thing to be done) we must make an effort to direct the minds of the people to the great subjects connected with their welfare. The main topic was the great salvation. At the same time the proper character and work of a missionary were described, the Scriptural character and influence of a Church were depicted. The importance of the education of the youth was stated and enforced, and an account of the numbers in our schools in this district was given and specimens of the children's ability exhibited. The progress of religion in our district, as evident in the attention of all the people to the means of grace, in the great increase of Church members, in the state of family religion and in the general moral-

65. Source: CWMA 213.
66. This was written during the Captaincy of the unpopular Abraham Kok, whose authority was disputed and who was often absent from Philippolis.

ity, industry and civilization of the whole population.

The real state of things in the Philippolis district was held up to view, its drunkenness and adult[er]y, its idleness, pride and marauding character, destitute of a government and of laws, without a school for the youth, a corrupt Church, the truth partially stated,[67] and that only to a few, and the important interests of a large population committed to the hands of one who had no character advantageously to influence nor heart to feel advantageously for their destinies. The consequence of this state of things to society and to individuals I hope many were enabled to see.

At the same time, to excite the jealousy of the people, a comparison was initiated between the moral condition and precepts of the Philippolis and Griqua Town districts, and now that God had sent them a man in Mr Atkinson who was devoted to their welfare, they were exhorted one and all to strengthen his hands and to encourage his heart by making the best of those means of improvement which God had now given them.

The people flocked in to the village from every part of the district to hear. Great numbers who had not been at church nor heard a sermon for three or four years came and heard, and we had crowded meetings during the five weeks I remained there. Through a blessing, it appeared that a deep impression was made, the people's attention seemed to be turned to important matters, and Mr Kolbe, who never entered the church himself, saw himself stripped of his last adherent. The respectable people were still determined to take advantage of the impression made; they sent him a message to request him to leave the district, which he did after some hesitation, and removed to the station of Mr Pellissier, about 60 or 70 miles distant, where he keeps a shop of general merchandise.

I would just remark further that in Mr Atkinson's letters to Dr Philip and the Directors there is abundance of circumstantial evidence against Mr K. in refference [*sic*] to the specific charges against him, and to attempt another investigation in order to a[s]certain the fact of his criminality, as matters now stand, would be highly improper, as such an attempt might be made use of, and that with effect, to produce again that state of ruinous excitement which would for some time at least be destructive of missionary opperations[?], and might be attended perhaps with more serious consequences to the peace and tranquil[l]ity of the country, as there exists no government or power to keep parties in check. Besides, you will be aware that in such a state of society, where there is no protection by a government on the one hand, nor strength of principle on the other, facts against an influential individual and the head of a strong party are not [to] be elicited and demolished by an investigation as they would be under an efficient and good government. Every individual who is known to possess a fact and is disposed to make a proper use of it is threatened and intimidated by the faction, and he knows that faithfulness will cost him his safety.[68]

It is no longer possible to judge the accusations against Kolbe and the subsequent developments in terms of guilt or innocence, and such considerations have, for that matter, long since become irrelevant. All that can be attempted is a brief summing up of the main factors as far as they can still be established.

In January 1836, after considerable delay, and under pressure from the Colonial authorities, Abraham Kok, the son of the late Adam Kok II, was elected Kaptyn, but the choice was not popular, and led to much dissension in the Captaincy. It was during the unsettled Captaincy of Abraham Kok that the charges of adultery were brought against Kolbe and that he was banished from the village. This was followed by the departure of Abraham Kok from Philippolis during the course of 1837, the election of his

---

67. "Sin was never spoken against" (note in the margin of the original).
68. The original letter ends abruptly with this statement.—Source of quotation: CWMA 214.

brother, Adam Kok III, as his successor, and a brief civil war during the winter of 1838, during which Abraham Kok and his uncle, Cornelius Kok II of Campbell, launched an attack on the village. The details of these developments are not clear, but here again the main division seems to have been between the Baster members of the congregation, as represented by the missionary Kolbe, and the Griquas led by Hendrik Hendrickze, a redoutable foe.

In this regard it is perhaps significant that not only were the Wieses members of the local congregation, but Elizabeth or Betta Wiese was a daughter of Jan Goeyman, the mission helper around whom the local Baster nucleus had originally formed at Philippolis, and various old loyalties and grievances were probably involved in the case. In May 1836, an anonymous traveller, passing through Philippolis wrote significantly of "the Griquas having accused the Bastards with plotting, in conjunction with Mr Colby [sic], their expulsion from the lands occupied by them".[69]

To this must be added the tensions produced the projected treaty with the British Government, which seems to have been violently opposed by the Griqua section of the community, and the intrigues of Dr Philip and Peter Wright to gain control of the developments in this regard.

In attempting to arrive at a fair assessment of the events at Philippolis during 1836, however, it is also necessary to remember that accusations of adultery were a standard weapon against missionaries.[70] If there were problems in the Kolbes' marriage, it would hardly have been surprising, for they had been married at 16, and now, at 33, were the parents of eight surviving children, the eldest of whom was a boy of 13 and the youngest an infant, while a baby had died the previous year at the age of four months. Since their appointment to Bushman Station in 1828, they had moreover been living on primitive and isolated mission stations in the far interior, and Philippolis, where they had been working for the past five years, was a deeply divided little community. Furthermore, most of the information about this particular case *that has survived comes from Atkinson and Wright, who seem to have been intensely prejudiced against Kolbe, and appear to have seen him as a threat to Dr Philip's plans for the Northern Frontier. Paradoxically enough, Kolbe therefore had not only Hendrickze and the Griqua party against him, but Philip, Wright and Atkinson as well, and in these circumstances his guilt or innocence were of little relevance.*

After his banishment from Philippolis, Kolbe seems to have remained in the Transgariep for some considerable time, living or visiting friends and supporters in the vicinity of Bethulie and Philippolis, and by 18 June 1838 Atkinson could still write to London:

I cannot say anything with certainty as to Mr K.'s intentions. He is still on this side of the river, though upwards of 50 miles from this place, but pays frequent visits to the house of Andries Wiese in this neighbourhood, and twice has remained above a fortnight. There have been various reports respecting his forming a new station, but there appears no definite prospect of its being carried into execution. Were such a thing to take place, there are some of the people, called Bastards, who would probably attach themselves to him, but I do not know any whose departure would be regretted, and their number is inconsiderable. At present Mr K. travels about as a trader.[71]

Kolbe eventually bought a farm between Bethulie and Burgersdorp, in the Colesberg district of the Cape Colony, where he died suddenly in 1844, at the age of 41, leaving a widow and ten surviving children.

69. *Cape Frontier Times* (22 12.1842).
70. In 1839 Atkinson would take part in an investigation of similar charges against J.P. Pellissier of the French mission station at Bethulie, and at the same time accusations of adultery were likewise made against Robert Moffat of Kuruman.
71. Source: CWMA 221.

5.
Theophilus Atkinson (1836–1840)

Theophilus Atkinson was an Englishman who with his wife, Henrietta Elizabeth Arderne, had accompanied Dr Philip on his return to South Africa in 1829, the intention being that they would be stationed on Madagascar. Local unrest having made this impossible, however, they were placed at the Cape, where they worked mainly at Bethelsdorp, before being transferred to Philippolis. "Mr Atkinson, who previously laboured at Bethelsdorp, has removed to this station," announced the annual report in 1837, "where, accompanied by Mrs Atkinson, he arrived on the 12th of last August [1836], after a difficult and fatiguing journey".[1] *No further mention was made of Kolbe.*

Atkinson, who was 31 at the time, emerges from his letters as a somewhat self-righteous and intolerant man, but his zeal for his work is undeniable, and moreover he communicated with the Directors in London with greater frequency and fluency than any of his predecessors, so that a comparatively full record of his sojourn on the station has been preserved. How fully he flung himself into his duties may be seen from his earliest surviving letter from Philippolis, dated 14 November 1836, which, while touching on his difficulties with Kolbe, who had recently left, deals mainly with the ordinary affairs of the mission, and it is quoted here at length as indication of what had been achieved there over thirteen years.

The services in which I am at present engaged are preaching on Saturday evenings and thrice on the Sabbath, besides attending the early morning prayer meeting, which has just been re-established, and a Sabbath school for adults, which I have now commenced. This, I hope, will be of great benefit to the people, comparatively few of whom are able to read the Scriptures.

During the week the forenoons are occupied with the school, which is yet but small, containing about 30 young persons and children. A considerable increase may, however, be expected after the harvest. There are no public services in the week, except on Saturday evenings, as the people very generally reside at a distance from the station on their respective farms, and at this season of the year there are only four or five families resident at the village.

The attendance on the Sabbath varies considerably. There is generally a numerous congregation once a fortnight, from 250 to 300, but on the intervening Sabbaths it is from 150 to 200. The number of the members of the Church is 38, and there are several candidates for admission.

From the abovementioned statement it will be seen that my time is fully occupied. And still an important part of my duties is left unfulfilled—that is, pastoral visitation. Scattered as the people here are over a great extent of country, they greatly need the itinerating labours of the missionary, and many require to be visited in order to be stirred up to a more diligent attendance on the public ordinances of religion. I am very desirous of doing this, but then the school must be neglected during my absence.There is also a considerable number of Bechuanas in various parts of the district, who are destitute of the means of grace, and if I had anyone to assist me, I would gladly do something likewise for their welfare. Two missionaries might with great advantage be

---

1. Report (1837), p.106.—The Atkinsons had two small daughters.

employed here, or if that cannot be, there should be a schoolmaster or assistant. Indeed, I ought to say two are necessary for the efficient discharge of the duties of this station. Mr Freeman did indeed authorise me to remain here with Mr Kolbe if we and our brethren thought it advisable. But this, I must candidly say, I cannot do, and I think the Directors will see from the documents before referred to that it is in every respect desirable that Mr Kolbe should not remain here. He has indeed resigned his duties at this station into my hands. I trust, however, that the circumstances of this field of labour will be taken into consideration, and that some assistance will either be sent me from England, or that Dr Philip will be authorised to endeavour to obtain an assistant for me in this country.

I have been authorised by Mr Freeman to build a house, on account of the state of the present mission house at this station, only to be economical. This I wish to be from principle. But building in this country is very expensive, owing to the want of timber and there being here no native builders. Mr F. did not specify any sum, and perhaps Mrs Philip may not feel herself authorised to allow me as much as will be required without the sanction of the Directors. I therefore mention the subject in this letter. From the estimates I have obtained, and my own calculations, I find the cost of a house on a very moderate scale will be about 1200 rixdollars or £190. The dimensions to be 37 ft by 22, one story, with cottage roof, and without ceiling or boarded floors. I mention this that it may be seen that I am not proceeding on an extravagant scale. And I hope the Directors will not object to the allowance of the requisite sum.

There is a garden adjoining that belonging to the mission, which Mr Kolbe would sell to the Society for £4 10s. This would be advantageous for another labourer at the station, should the Directors think proper to purchase it. On this as well as the other topics of this communication I shall be glad to have a reply as early as possible. I am at present occupying a house belonging to one of the people, which I have hired for a time, but it is by no means a comfortable one, and I must get the new one as fast as possible.[2]

By 30 June 1837 Atkinson, after having dealt in his letter to London with the further developments concerning Kolbe,[3] could report considerable progress.

The public services of the Sabbath continue the same in number as when I last wrote, but are somewhat different in their character. In December [1836] I commenced preaching to the Bechuanas through an interpreter on the Sabbath afternoon. At first about 60 attended, but they soon increased to upwards of 200, and continued about that number till lately that the cold weather has diminished their attendance, most of them having to come from distant places. It is with great pleasure and thankfulness I inform you that this attempt appears to be graciously owned of God for the salvation of several individuals.

At first I felt a good deal discouraged. I could only speak through an interpreter, and I found that he did not translate faithfully what was said, and I thought little or no good would be done unless I could get the language and speak directly to the people. However, I determined to go on, as the poor Bechuanas shewed a great desire to hear the Word of God, and I had no other means of doing anything for their spiritual benefit. And, as in many other instances, God has been pleased to bless the weakest means for the accomplishemt of the great purposes of His grace. There are 18 of these people, most of whom never heard the Gospel before, now anxiously inquiring after the way of salvation, and affording pleasing hope that the work of grace is begun in their hearts. Among them is my interpreter, who is evidently

2. Source: CWMA 209.
3. See pp.94–96 above.

improved in spirit (being much more humble), and likewise in the manner of his interpreting; and I hope he will yet become increasingly useful.

On the Sabbath evening I have lately at the request of several persons who could not so well understand the Dutch had the sermon translated into the Hottentot language, and thus as in the afternoon with the Bechuanas, those who could not otherwise understand what was spoken may now do so, while all have the benefit of it as it is delivered in Dutch.[4]

I have not found it advisable as yet to increase the number of public services in the week, but Mrs Atkinson has for some time held a Bible class for the females on Wednesday afternoons, and I have one on Thursdays for all who choose to attend. In the former the New Testament is read, in the latter the Old Testament. Though but few can read, many attend for the purpose of hearing what is read and the remarks that are made. These classes, we hope, will be benificial in imparting a knowledge of the Holy Scriptures, in which the people are lamentably deficient. The adult school on the Sabbath will, I trust, ultimately conduce to the same end. It is generally well attended, in the summer about 150 remained to be taught in it, but now the shortness of the days prevents many of them from doing so.

I continue to conduct the day school every forenoon. The attendance at the time of my last report was 30; it is now, I am happy to say, generally from 120 to 130, and sometimes above 140. It is composed of men, women and children, about three fifths of whom are Bechuanas. Nearly the whole of the number were at first in the alphabet, but most of them are now spelling, and some are beginning to read. The want of a suitable schoolroom prevents their being taught to write, with the exception of 10 or 12, and also their being taught on the British system.[5] But this difficulty will, I hope, be removed in a few months, when the new schoolhouse shall be finished.

Monday is fully occupied with speaking with the candidates,

except during the school hours, as I am obliged to have them with me on this day on account of those who must go to their farms at a distance. In the afternoon I hold a meeting in the chapel for those candidates who understand Dutch, and have the Bechuanas at my house. Those of the Bechuana inquirers who reside here are with me almost every day to converse about their spiritual state. One person was admitted to church fellowship this month, and I hope before the close of the year to have the privilege of adding to their numbers. It has been found necessary to exclude several from the Church for long-continued neglect of the Lord's Supper and an improper spirit. This, though a painful measure, will, I trust, be for the ultimate good of the Church.

The missionary prayer meetings continue to be well attended. Mrs Atkinson has also formed a Maternal Association, which meets on the same day. It is at present only in its infancy, and we cannot tell how it will succeed. (…)

I have still reason to be thankful to the Author of all our mercies for a continuance of health to my dear family and myself. I felt the various services rather too much in the hot weather, and my dear wife complained of great weakness, but now that the weather is cold I have nothing to complain of, and my dear partner will, I hope, improve in health.

I feel obliged by your readiness in allowing the grant for the house and garden. I regret that the building has been delayed for want of timber, but as the other material is ready, it will not be long in building when once commenced. I shall do my best as it regards economy, but if it should somewhat exceed the sum allowed, I trust it will be kindly excused. In the meantime our personal accommodations are rather more comfortable than they were last winter, as we have now a glass window, by which the

---

4. The "Hottentot language" was most likely Xiri, the Khoi language commonly spoken among the Griquas.
5. By means of monitors chosen from amongst the more advanced pupils.

cold winds are excluded, while daylight is enjoyed. It has, however, been intensely cold for a few days since I began this letter, and it was with some difficulty that I could hold my pen. It is now the 5th July; on the 1st we had the scenery of an English winter, the ground being covered with snow. I have been unavoidably prevented from dispatching this so soon as I intended.

I should feel obliged if you would send me some millboards for mounting the school lessons; we cannot get suitable planks for that purpose here. They can be sent out whole or in halves, but packed in a case. Be so kind as to send it direct to Algoa Bay, to the care of Messrs Hough, who will forward it to me. (…)

As I am very frequently obliged to give out medicine among the people, I would be obliged if the Directors would be so kind as to send me a small quantity of the common [*illegible*] such as jalap, rhubarb, ipecacuanha, James powder, &c &c. Also sulphate of quinine.

I am also in need of writing paper for the school, and as it [is] much cheaper in England than here, it would be an advantage to have a ream or two of foolscap, the yellow wove is preferable for school purposes to the other sort. It would be advisable to send some packing paper (2 or 3 quires) for making covers for the copy-books, or any other paper would answer the same purpose.[6]

Besides his various and varied duties at Philippolis, however, Atkinson, like his predecessors, also itinerated in the district, and like them sent a journal of his travels to the Directors of the LMS in London. The following extract describes his first itinerating journey, undertaken in the winter of 1837.

I mentioned in my last[7] the importance of itinerating in the distant parts of this district. The great increase of the school and the backward state of the children made me unwilling to leave the station and allow the school to be suspended. But the circumstances of the people, living as they were utterly regardless of the public ordinances of religion, determined me on taking a journey among them for a few days, and I beg leave to subjoin a few of the notes taken on this tour.[8]

May 9 [1837]. I left home for an excursion among the Griquas, with a view to stir them up to attend to their spiritual and eternal interests. Could not reach any farm that night. Spanned out in an open plain. Weather cold and rainy.

May 10. After several hours' ride over a flat and uninteresting country, I came to the farm of one of the Griquas, and found a considerable number of people there from another fountain. I persuaded[9] them to remain a little while, and held a short service. Spoke to them on Hebrews 9:27.[10] All were eager for tracts or spelling books. Gave them as many as I could spare, and some sheet lessons for the school at Toom Fountain,[11] to which most of them belonged.

Rode on to a large kraal of Bechuanas. About 60 sat round the fire by my waggon, and I spoke to them from John 3:16.[12] Having my Bechuana interpreter and another who is also an inquirer for my driver and leader. Spent some time after the service talking with those that remained, and had a pleasant evening with them.[13]

6. Source: CWMA 213–214.
7. His letters of 24 & 27.1.1837; CWMA 213 & 214.
8. The journal was published, with some emendations, in the *Evangelical Magazine* XVI (1838), pp.358–9. The more striking of the editorial changes will, as a matter of interest, be indicated in the footnotes. In this case, the scriptural references will also be supplied in the footnotes.
9. "Invited" in the published text.
10. "And as it is appointed unto men once to die, but after this the judgment...".
11. Toomfontein, between modern Trompsburg and Edenburg.
12. "And no man hath ascended up to heaven, but he that came down from heaven."
13. In the published version, "talking" in the above sentence became "conversing", and "pleasant" was turned into the more edifying "interesting".

May 11. Very cold with hoar frost. However, the people assembled again, and before starting I addressed them from John 3:3.[14] They listened very attentively. They are too far from Philippolis to attend divine service there, consequently they had many of them never heard anything of the Gospel before. May some lasting good result from this interview!

Went to Round Fountain.[15] Spent some time in talking with the candidates for church fellowship who were residing there. In the afternoon visited the school, which is conducted by a Bechuana baptised in Cape Town, and who has taken the name of Richard Miles.[16] There were 27 children present, and I was on the whole pleased with the manner in which the school was conducted. After the school the people assembled for divine service; about 40 present. Spoke to them from Ezekiel 18:31.[17]

I am sorry to be obliged to add that shortly after my return home this place was let to a farmer from the Colony, in consequence of which the people residing there were obliged to remove, and the school was broken up. The teacher as well as most of the people are at present unsettled; but I may perhaps be able to make some arrangement for his being again employed.

May 11. Had worship in the school before leaving. Read and expounded part of Luke 15.[18] Gave tracts to those who could read, and left some lessons for the school. Observed that the locusts have made sad ravages over the country through which I was travelling.

Arrived a little before sunset at a place where there were several kraals of Griquas. In the evening had service in one of the houses (the round mat houses of the country). About 40 were in and about the house. Spoke to them on Matt.16:26,[19] endeavouring to shew them the immense value of their souls and the importance of seeking their salvation.

This evening is the Missionary Communion in London. Many prayers are now being offered to God for missionaries and for the heathen. O that this ignorant and careless people[20] may receive a share of the blessings implored!

May 13. Finding that this place was surrounded with other kraals, and that I could collect a large congregation on the Sabbath, I concluded on remaining here till Monday. Talked with the people about having their children instructed,[21] and at length found a young man who was willing to undertake the duty. Gave him some sheet lessons, and spelling books to a few who were eager to learn.

Walked to another kraal about 3 miles distant. After a little conversation with them, I requested them to attend the services on the following day, which they promised to do. In the evening had family worship in one of the houses. Read and expounded part of John 4.[22]

May 14, Sabbath. I was not disappointed in expecting a considerable number would assemble. Upwards of 200 were present at the morning and afternoon services. They appeared very attentive. I preached in the morning from Luke 13:3, and in the afternoon from 1 Tim.4:8.[23] After the afternoon service most of the people left for their respective places. Gave tracts to a few who could read. In the evening held the service in the house (the two former having been held in the open air). About 50 were

---

14. "Except a man be born again, he cannot see the kingdom of God."
15. Rondefontein, immediately to the north of the modern town of Springfontein
16. After the missionary who had acted in the place of Dr Philip during the latter's visit to England in 1826–29.
17. "Cast away from you all your transgressions."
18. The parables of the Good Shepherd and the Prodigal Son.
19. "For what is a man profited, if he shall gain the whole world, and lose his own soul?"
20. "Poor and ignorant" in the published version.
21. "Admonished the people to have their children instructed" in the published version.
22. The story of Jesus and the Samaritan woman.
23. "Except ye repent, ye shall all likewise perish"; and "Godliness is profitable unto all things".

present, but not half could get inside. Spoke to them on Matt.21:29.[24] I endeavoured in all the services to speak with plainness and earnestness. Most of the hearers, I hope, understood, O, that these attempts may not have been in vain!

The pleasure I felt in having this opportunity of making known the way of salvation to those who seldom or never had heard anything of the kind was considerably damped by the thought that my flock and family at the station were left destitute, and must pass a silent Sabbath. But I trust they have remembered me at the Throne of Grace, and that both they and I will have reason to be thankful to God for this day.

May 15. Set off early for Uitkomst, the farthest place I intended to visit, and arrived there about noon.[25] Found but few people there, many having removed and some being temporarily absent. Held service in the afternoon, and spoke on Acts 16:30,31.[26] Between 30 and 40 were present. Furnished the teacher, a young woman, with some lessons for the children. Had many applications for spelling books, and gave away all I had left, and a few tracts.

I intended to have had another service in the evening, but a report arrived that a great number of horsemen armed with guns were not far off, and this so frightened the people that they all determined on removing to a neighbouring Coranna kraal for the night, there being then only two men at home. Though I did not place any credit in the report, yet as all the people were leaving, I thought it would be useless for me to remain, and accordingly accompanied the fugitives, and all arrived at the place of refuge late in the evening. There was too much confusion to allow of collecting the people together. I therefore deferred it till a night's rest should have somewhat composed them.

May 16. Found that the alarm had quite subsided, and that the Uitkomst people were preparing to return home. However, I got them together with several Corannas, about 60 in all. I first reminded the former how glad they were to find a place of refuge when there was only the report of danger, and how much more necessary it was that they should seek refuge for their souls, where the danger was real and awful, and pointed out to them Christ as their only refuge. Afterwards I spoke to all on John 3:7.[27]

Immediately after the service the other waggons left the place, and I set my face again towards home. Rode to one of the kraals that I had visited on the Saturday (13th), and spanned out at 2 p.m. The people came together at my request, and I addressed them on 1 John 3:20.[28] About 30 present. Left that place again about 4, and rode till late at night: the weather clear and frosty, but the moon being near the full made it pleasant.[29] The dry brown grass presented the appearance of a field of snow.

May 17. Rode to Schiet Fountain,[30] where I found the people busy treading out corn (with horses). As they could not well leave their work, I stayed that night there and had service in the evening. Spoke on Heb. 2:3.[31] Seventeen persons present.[32] Found several who could read, and gave them tracts.

May 18. Called at another fountain on my way home, but found no-one there except a few Bechuanas who were left in charge of the place. After a little conversation with them through my interpreter, I left them and came on to Philippolis, where I arrived in safety soon after sunset, happy and thankful to find my dear family well, and welcomed by those of the people who

24. "He answered and said, I will not; but afterward he repented, and went."
25. Between modern Edenburg and Petrusburg, some 80km to the north of Philippolis.
26. "Believe on the Lord Jesus Christ, and thou shalt be saved."
27. "Marvel not that I said unto thee, ye must be born again."
28. "For every one that doeth evil hateth the light."
29. In the published text this oddly enough became, "but the soft radiance of the moon made it pleasant".
30. Some 30 km north-west of Philippolis.
31. "How shall we escape, if we neglect so great salvation."
32. Omitted in the published text.

reside here. May this journey be followed with beneficial and lasting effects, and conduct to the salvation of many souls.

I had generally very fine weather for that season during my journey, otherwise I could not have held so many services in the open air as was the case in most instances. I should be very glad to be employed more in these itinerating duties, could I do so without detriment to the station. And I do hope, honoured Brethren, that you will as soon as possible enable me to spend more time in this way by providing me with a fellow-labourer.[33]

By the end of the year further upheavals had been caused at Philippolis by the struggle for the succession to the Captaincy,[34] and various other temporal setbacks had also to be reported to London in Atkinson's survey of 1837.

The number of baptisms has been 11, viz. one adult and 10 children. Marriages 13, 7 of which were Bechuana couples. The burials have been 10, viz. 3 adults and 7 infants. There has been a great deal of sickness this year, especially among the children. Five of the above died in the month of July. In many instances then, and also more recently, by the Divine blessing on the timely use of means, the fever was cut short and the lives of the children preserved. I have had numerous applications for medicine, and therefore hope that my request to be supplied with a few of the simple medicines will be kindly acceded to. Ipecacuanha powder has been one of the most useful, and my stock is nearly exhausted.

The people have contributed this year £10 to the funds of the Society. There has been some demand for Bibles, which I have only been able partially to meet, on account of the difficulty of get them conveyed from Cape Town to this distant station. Nine have been sold, and nine Testaments. Tracts have been also from time to time distributed.

In regard to secular concerns, this year has been in most

respects a very trying one. I have already referred to the drought, which has been long and severe, and which has occasioned a great loss to the people in cattle. The Lord has, however, at length remembered us in mercy. In several parts of the district copious rains have lately fallen, and last evening we had an abundant rain here. We have often now a literal accomplishment of the threatening, "The Lord shall make the rain of thy land powder and dust." The clouds have very often risen and seemed to promise abundance of rain, but it has ended in a storm of wind and dust, completely filling and darkening the atmosphere. In addition to the drought, the land was overrun with locusts, which destroyed all the corn, except at two places, one of which is the Society's, where my corn was sown, and which is thus mercifully preserved amidst the general devastation.[35] This distinguishing mercy of our Heavenly Father calls upon us for renewed gratitude and devotedness to His service.

I have not been able to perform any itinerating journey since I wrote last. The extreme barrenness of the country and the weakness of my oxen would have made it impracticable, even had not the disturbed state of affairs rendered it inexpedient.[36] But besides this, I may say that I have been so fully employed here that I could not have left home. Independent of the works of the mission, I have been of necessity much occupied in building. I have had a great deal of trouble in getting the new schoolhouse thatched, and now, owing to the existing state of the country, the work is again standing still, and will yet cost considerable labours before it is completed.

The superintending of the building of our new dwelling house has likewise occupied much of my time. Owing to the long delay

33. Source: CWMA 213–214.
34. See pp.103–104 above.
35. Presumably Boesmansfontein; see p.25 above.
36. This refers to the struggle for the Captaincy between Abraham Kok and Adam Kok III.

in the bringing of the timber from the Kat River, the building was not commenced till the end of August, and even then it was only in the hope of the speedy arrival of the timber, which, however, was not brought till nearly the end of October. Since that time the work has been going on better, but its progress has not been so satisfactory as I could wish. The workmen are now engaged in thatching, two of the inner partitions are carried up, and most of the carpenter's work is done, so that I hope in a few weeks longer to see it finished.

But I must now come to the least pleasant part of the subject. I had by a rough calculation estimated the cost of the building at £90, which the Directors were so kind as to allow. I regret to state that it will very considerably exceed that sum. It was remarked in your letter of 23rd March in reference to this grant that if the house could be completed for that sum without detriment to the building, it would be so much the more pleasing. It would indeed have been gratifying to me to have been able to effect this, but I could not under the circumstances in which I am placed. Had it been possible to obtain timber in the Great River,[37] within a moderate distance, this would have lessened the immediate outlay, but then it would not have lasted half the time that the yellowwood will, as in a few years it is destroyed by worms. The building is now strong and durable, but of the plainest possible description throughout. No expence has been incurred that was not absolutely necessary. There are no superfluities, not even what is deemed indispensable in almost every house in England, viz. a ceiling and a floor. The house is open to the thatch, and the floor will be of clay. The doors are all of the plainest kind, none of them being panelled. And the glazing and painting I shall do myself.

I mention these particulars to show that I have done my utmost as regards economy, and have been scrupulously careful of lavishing the funds of the Society. Where I had erred in my calculations was in the quantity and the price of the timber it would take, and the expence of the carpenter's work. For instance, the beams I had expected to get for 12s each, and they cost 18s. It has also been longer in hand that I had anticipated, which of course has increased the item of labourers' wages. (...)[38]

In conclusion I beg leave to repeat my earnest wishes to be favoured with a colleague on this mission as soon as possible. I have hitherto been enabled through Divine goodness to sustain all the labours of the station. But I am anxious to give greater efficiency to the measures in operation by itinerating to the distant kraals.[39]

By the winter of 1838 a certain degree of stability had returned to the congregation at Philippolis, although Kolbe was still "on this side of the river"[40] and Atkinson was corresponding with the Directors in London about the ownership of his farm Driefontein,[41] and the struggle for the Captaincy had moreover been resolved in favour of Adam Kok III. At this time Atkinson, who had now been stationed here for two years, wrote as follows to London.

I am thankful to be able to inform you that the decrease in the attendance at public worship and the school was, as I hoped, very temporary.[42] A great number of the Griquas came shortly after with their families to reside on the station, and from that time to the present, with two or three exceptions, our place of

37. The Orange.
38. Atkinson enclosed with this letter a sketch and plan of a five-roomed house measuring 40 by 22 feet, with a kitchen at the back, the external walls being 9 feet high, together with a calculation of expenses amounting to £132 19s.
39. Source: CWMA 217 (25.12.1837)
40. See p.105 above.
41. The farm had been bought by Kolbe from his predecessor Melvill, and was sold after his departure from Philippolis to the widow of Adam Kok II.
42. This refers to the figures quoted in his previous letter (25.12.1837).

worship has been filled, and often crowded. Most of these people had been living for years in the neglect of the ordinances of the Gospel. Some of them I visited on my journey last year, but so completely have the political changes affected the general state of things that I should perhaps not find six families were I to take the same circuit again.

It is encouraging to see so many of them brought once more under the sound of the Gospel, and I cannot but indulge the hope that this is a token that the Lord has yet purposes of mercy towards this people. There are some who were formerly connected with the Church under Mr Anderson's care,[43] who have for a long period been wanderers from the fold, but who now seem desirous of returning to the Shepherd and Bishop of their souls. A few of these attend the weekly meetings that I hold with inquirers. It will indeed be a great privilege to be instrumental in gathering up some of the scattered remains of my venerable brother's labours in this land, and preparing them for that blessed world where both he that soweth and he that reapeth shall rejoice together.

The day school under my care has been for some time well attended. I have, however, been disappointed of the convenience of another schoolroom. The one I mentioned before as being partly thatched fell down about the end of March, after a heavy rain, the walls being built of clay and proving too weak to support the weight of the roof. Providentially no lives were lost, though some children who were at play within the walls at the time were much bruised. Had it occurred a few weeks later, it would have been occupied, and the consequences might have been dreadful. Dr Philip has authorised me to build a more substantial [school]house, and has agreed to advance £100 for this purpose on account of the Society. I shall do my best to get it built as economically as possible.[44]

In February an infant school was opened, which contains about 70 children. Mrs Atkinson is assisted in it by a pious young woman from Port Elizabeth who now resides here. The building used for this school is the old mission house, which though not very convenient, answers the purpose at present.

On February 4th I had the privilege of baptising and receiving into the Church four of the Bechuanas, the first fruits among that nation in the mission. I trust many more of them will in due time be added to the Lord. Among the other people, five have been received. There are two classes of candidates, one consisting of Griquas and others who speak the Dutch language, of whom there are 18, and the other of Bechuanas, who are at present 29. Twenty-seven who attended this class have left the place at different times and have removed to other missionary stations. It would have been gratifying to have been allowed to watch the progress of these individuals, who received their first serious impressions here, and I much regret the departure of some of them, but I trust they will go on well under the care of my esteemed brethren at the several places where they now reside.

There has been a great deal of sickness in the village and the district for several months past. It is a species of fever of a very lingering nature, but it has not proved fatal in any instance as far as I am aware. With gratitude to the Heavenly Father I would add that we have been preserved in good health amidst the surrounding disease. I have had a constant demand on my medicine, and the stock of the necessary articles is almost exhausted, such[?] as ipecacuanha, jalop, calomel, tartar emetic and rhubarb. I hope therefore that the supply requested in a former letter have been kindly granted and forwarded.

43. This refers to the beginnings of the mission at Klaarwater (Griquatown).
44. The responsibility for the erection this building being taken over by Gottlob Schreiner after his arrival on the station at the end of 1838, it had still not been completed at the time of Dr Philip's visit to the station four years later.

Our new dwelling-house is, I am happy to say, at length finished, and we are now living in comparative comfort. We are now able to have a fire, which we could not before, but which is very necessary at this season of the year, when the frost is often severe.

I was exceedingly glad, beloved Brethren, to be assured of your intention to send me a fellow-labourer in this mission. But from Dr Philip's remarks on this point there seems to be a great uncertainty as to when he may be expected. Allow me to repeat the hope that it may not be very long. From the favourable change lately manifested among the Griquas it does appear that now is the time to make a vigorous effort for their good by a system of well-directed operation. And this cannot be done when the missionary has to work single-handed in a field as widely extended as this is. The encouragement already experienced among the Bechuanas is likewise of manifest call of Divine Providence to do something more for the welfare of that people.

I am aware of the difficulty of procuring suitable labourers, for during most of the time that I was in the College there were only twelve or thirteen of us.[45] And now on looking over a list of twenty-eight with whom I was more or less connected, I find but ten now employed in the missionary field, all the rest having either been prevented from entering it or subsequently removed from it. I have reason therefore for peculiar gratitude to God, who has thus favoured me above so many, and desire to devote all my energies to His service. It is not that I may have less work that I am anxious for a colleague, but that more may be done in this important field of exertion, and I trust, Brethren, that you will not lose sight of the pressing wants of the mission. For some time to come all that is to be done must be done by the missionaries. We are in this respect very far behind some of the Churches in this part of the world.[46] There are no individuals whom I could employ as yet as native teachers. This is a deficiency which cannot be a matter of surprise, considering the great disadvantages under which the mission has laboured. Pray for us, beloved Brethren, that a great revival of the work of the Lord may take place among us.[47]

The fellow-labourer repeatedly requested by Atkinson was to make his appearance all too soon in the shape of a newly-ordained young German, Gottlob Schreiner, who had accompanied Philip on the latter's return from his second visit to England in 1837, and who arrived at Philippolis with his wife Rebecca in December 1838.[48] He took responsibility mainly for the work among the Batswana on the station; but he was an extremely stubborn and self-willed young man, and within six months the quarrels of the two missionaries were generally known in mission circles. Unfortunately for Atkinson his zeal in driving Kolbe from the station had made him extremely unpopular with the Baster section of the community, who formed the core of his congregation, and the dissension between the two men was exploited to drive him away in turn. In 1840, after a great deal of acrimony and uncertainty, he left the station and settled at Colesberg, where he worked among the Coloured people for several years, but he was ultimately to spend the greater part of his long life at Pacaltsdorp in the Cape Colony, dying there in 1852.

Schreiner for his part soon antagonised the local community of Philippolis by his tactless behaviour, his mismanagement of the rebuilding of the school and his obvious preference for the

45. The College of the LMS in Hoxton, London.
46. Both the Wesleyans and the Paris Missionary Society made extensive use of "local preachers" and other indigenous assistants, but under the influence mainly of Robert Moffat a strong feeling had developed in the LMS against "native agents" and similar missionary workers such as Jan Goeyman had been.
47. Source: CWMA 221 (19.6.1838).
48. The appointment seems to have been made in July, but Schreiner was apparently in no great hurry to set out for the interior, in spite of having received a "very pressing letter" from Atkinson; see Schreiner, p.29.

more docile Batswana, and more specifically incurred the enmity of the Kaptyn and Raad. In these circumstances he was was a serious impediment to Philip's plan to acquire control of the Griqua states, and was summarily dismissed on the occasion of the Doctor's visit to the Transorange in 1842.[49] *The fact that he was succeeded by Peter Wright of Griquatown, Philip's right hand in the implemenation of his grand Griqua policy, is an indication of the importance Philippolis had attained within twenty years of its establishment.*

49. He established a new station among the Basotho at Basel, near the Caledon River, but it was not a great success, and in 1846 he resigned to join the Wesleyan Missionary Society.

Chronology

1801
The LMS begins an itinerating mission to the population along the middle Orange River

1804
December, a permanent Baster mission established at Klaarwater

1813
August, the Basters adopt the name Griquas and Klaarwater becomes Griquatown

1820
First mention of a school for Bushmen established by the LMS at Ramah under Piet Sabba and Andries Pretorius

1821
Bergenaar rebels leave Griquatown

1822
A school for the Bushmen of the Transgariep established by the LMS at Philippolis under Jan Goeyman
A Baster settlement gradually comes into being at Philippolis

1825
August, visit of Dr Philip to Philippolis; James Clark placed here to take charge of the station

Meeting of Philip with Adam Kok II and followers, and with the Bergenaars

November, Goeyman leaves Philippolis

1826

10 January, the election of Adam Kok II as Kaptyn approved by the British authorities

Peter Wright of Griquatown on behalf of Dr Philip gives Adam Kok II and his followers permission to settle in the Philippolis area

May, massacre of the inhabitants of Boesmansfontein in a retaliatory attack by "Caffres" after a cattle raid

James Clark summons Adam Kok II to Philippolis

22 July, Clark cedes the mission station to Adam Kok II

Adam Kok II resigns in favour of his son, Cornelius Kok III

1827

10 January, John Melvill arrives at Philippolis as missionary

December, journey of exploration by Clark and Melvill to determine on a new station for the Bushmen

1828

28 February, G.A.Kolbe accepted as a missionary by the LMS

March, Bushman School (Bethulie) established by Clark; Kolbe appointed to work here with him

November, journey of exploration by Melvill and Kolbe to the Caledon River valley

Death of Cornelis Kok III; Adam Kok II resumes the office of Kaptyn

1829

February, the settlement at Philippolis moved temporarily to Boesmansfontein

1831
13 March, G.A. Kolbe arrives at Philippolis to take over the station from Melvill

1833
26 May, Kolbe ordained at Philippolis by visiting French missionaries

1834
July, Bushman School abandoned by the LMS and the station handed over to the PMS

1835
12 September, death of Adam Kok II

1836
26 January, Abraham Kok elected Kaptyn
Kolbe accused of adultery
12 August, Theophilus Atkinson arrives at Philippolis
November, Kolbe leaves the station

1837
7 January, meeting of Abraham Kok with Andries Stockenstrom, Lieutenant-Governor of the Eastern Province, on the Orange River
January, Kolbe expelled from Philippolis by Abraham Kok and Raad
25 February, treaty concluded between Abraham Kok and Andries Waterboer
September, Barend Lucas briefly acts as Kaptyn
Adam Kok III elected Kaptyn

1838
Winter: Griqua "civil war"; Abraham Kok formally deposed

9 November, treaty concluded between Adam Kok III and Waterboer

7 December, Gottlob Schreiner arrives at Philippolis

Suggested further reading

For the general history of the LMS, see Richard Lovett, *The history of the London Missionary Society, 1795–1896* (London: H. Frowde, 1899); and for individual missionaries, James Sibree, *A register of missionaries, deputations, etc.*; 4th ed. (London: LMS, 1923). Information on Dr Philip and his involvement in the political affairs of his day may be found in William Miller Macmillan, *Bantu, Boer and Briton* (London: Faber & Gwyer, 1929); and Andrew Ross, *John Philip, 1775–1851* (Aberdeen: Aberdeen University Press, 1986).

For the beginning of the mission to the Bushmen in general, see Karel Schoeman, *J.J. Kicherer en die vroeë sending, 1799–1806* (Cape Town: S.A. Library, 1996). For the earliest mission stations for this group, see two articles by the same author, "Die Londense Sendinggenootskap en die San: die stasies Toornberg en Hephzibah, 1814–1818", *S.A. Historical Journal* 28 (1993); and "Die Londense Sendinggenootskap en die San: die stasies Ramah, Konnah en Philippolis, 1816–1828", *ibid.* 29 (1993).

An account of developments at Philippolis subsequent to the arrival of Gottlob Schreiner is to be found in an earlier publication in the *Vrijstatia* series, *The missionary letters of Gottlob Schreiner, 1837–46*; ed. Karel Schoeman (Cape Town: Human & Rousseau, 1991).

The *Dictionary of South African Biography (DSAB)* contains articles on John Philip and Peter Wright (vol.I), and John Melvill (vol.IV), all with sources. An article on the life and work of Jan

Goeyman is to be found in Karel Schoeman, *The early mission in South Africa, 1799–1819* (Pretoria: Protea Book House, 2005). *South African genealogies* by Heese & Lombard provides genealogical information on Theophilus Atkinson (vol.1), Goeyman (vol.2), G.A. Kolbe (vol.4) and Melvill (vol.5).

J. du Plessis, *A history of the Christian missions in South Africa* (London: Longmans, Green, 1911) is a comprehensive survey of this subject, but very much out of date.

For the history of the Griqua Captaincy of Philippolis in a broader context, consult Martin Legassick, *The Griquas, the Sotho-Tswana and the Missionaries* (Ann Arbor, Mich.: University Microfilms, 1986); the standard work on the Griquas is Robert Ross, *Adam Kok's Griquas* (London: Cambridge University Press, 1976). For the Philippolis Captaincy specifically, see *Griqua Records: the Philippolis Captaincy, 1826–1861*; ed. Karel Schoeman (Cape Town: Van Riebeeck Society, 1996), which is a collection of official documents; and Karel Schoeman, *The Griqua Captaincy of Philippolis, 1826–1861* (Pretoria: Protea Book House, 2002), a socio-cultural and historical survey. The *DSAB* (vol.IV) has articles on Adam Kok II and Adam Kok III. All these works list further sources of information.

Contemporary accounts by visitors to Philippolis and the Captaincy during the period covered here may be found most notably in *The diary of Andrew Smith, 1834–36;* ed. Percival R. Kirby (Cape Town: Van Riebeeck Society, 1939–40); *Andrew Smith's journal of his expedition into the interior of South Africa, 1834–36*; ed. William F. Lye (Cape Town: A.A. Balkema, 1975); and James Backhouse, *A narrative of a visit to the Mauritius and South Africa* (London: Hamilton, Adams, & Co., 1844).

Index

admission to church membership, *see* church membership:admissions
adultery, 16, 102; as charge against missionaries, 104, 105 n70; allegations against G.A. Kolbe, 82–105 *passim*
Afrikaans language, 43 n20
agriculture, *see references under* farming
alcohol, *see* liquor trade; intemperance
Algoa Bay, 112
amaNdebele, *see* Ndebele tribe
amaThembu, *see* Thembu people
amaXhosa, *see* Xhosa people
Anderson, William, 75, 122
Arbousset, Thomas, 79 n35, 80
arms and ammunition, 11, 61–62 *passim*
associations, *see* church associations
Atkinson, Henrietta Elizabeth (Arderne), 106, 111, 122–123, 110
Atkinson, Theophilus, 105 n70, 106; appointment, 83, 86, 93, 106; as correspondent, 106; and G.A. Kolbe, 83–105 *passim*, 106, 108, 109, 121, 125; P. Wright's opinion of him, 98; praised by Raad, 102; departure, 125; death, 125
Auxiliary Mission Society: Cape Town, 67 n5, 70; Philippolis, 66, 81, 118

backsliding (religious), *see* religious life (personal)
baptismal candidates, *see* candidates for baptism and church membership
baptisms, 73, 81, 82, 118, 123
Barends, Barend, 77 n25
Barkly West, 95 n56
barley cultivation, 63
barter, *see* trading and barter
Bartlett, John, 17
Basel (mission), 126 n49
Basotho, *see* Sotho people
Baster community (Philippolis), 27, 31, 34, 58, 60; establishment, 13, 23, 37; and settlement of Philippolis by Griquas, 22–35 *passim*; J. Clark proposed as 'Captain', 32; support for J. Melvill, 46–47; support for G.A. Kolbe, 92, 104, 105, 125
Basutos, *see* Sotho people
Batlhaping, *see* Tlhaping tribe
Batlokwa, *see* Tlokwa tribe ('Mantatees')
Batswana, see Tswana people
beads, 39
Bechuanas, *see* Tswana people
Berends, Berend, *see* Barends, Barend
Berg River, 83 n40
Bergenaars, 13, 15 n18, 17–18, 22, 26, 29, 34, 38–39, 47 n26, 48(2x), 50, 61 n57
Berlin Missionary Society, 75, 76, 95 n56
Bethanie (mission), 76
Bethelsdorp (mission), 10, 26, 28–29, 32–33, 37, 41, 83, 106
Bethulie (mission), 35, 76; G.A. Kolbe

here, 102–105 *passim*
Bible study, 38, 107, 110
Bibles, 82, 118
blacksmiths, 83 n41, 89 n47
Bloem, Jan, 94
Bly Vooruitzicht, 9
Boers, 22, 29, 31, 42, 53, 114; and missionaries, 12, 52, 53, 53, 70, 73 *passim*; conflict with Griquas, 68; women, 54
Boesmansfontein, 18, 41 n13; as mission farm, 25; settlement at Philippolis moved here, 58, 60; raid (1826), 23–26 *passim*, 30
Boetsap, 69 n9, 77 n25
books, *see* reading matter
Bootschap (mission), *see* Buchuaap
Bothitong, 79 n35
Bourke, Richard, Sir, 35
brandy, 72, 85
brandy trade, *see* liquor trade
brickmaking, 16
British Resident (Transgariep), 87 n46
British Settlers (1820), 65
British system (schools), 110
Buchuaap (mission), 73
building (general), 23, 30, 84
building costs, 108, 120–121
building materials, 122. *See also* glass windows; timber.
buildings (Philippolis), *see* church building; mission house; school building
Burgersdorp, 105
burials, 118
Bushman Country (name), 34
Bushman School (mission), *see* Bushman Station
Bushman Station (mission), 35, 62, 65, 76, 84, 104, 79 n35, 104. *See also* Bethulie.
Bushmen, 13; original owner of fountain at Philippolis, 41; children, 42, 55: food, 12; cattle raiding, 40–41, 44–45, 70; in service of Boers, 55. *See also* mission to Bushmen.

'Caffres' (generic term), 17–18, 19, 29–31 *passim*, 34, 48, 50; raid on Boesmansfontein, 23–26 *passim*
Caledon Institution (mission), *see* Bushman Station
Caledon River, 23, 33, 126 n49
Caledon River valley, 76
Campbell (mission), 17 n27, 48
Campbell, John, 9–10, 11
Campbell Captaincy, 22, 89, 104
candidates for baptism and church membership, 66, 69, 78, 81, 82, 107, 110–111, 123
Cape Colony: treaties with Captaincies, 82, 94, 97–98, 99, 104. *See also* Government Agent; passes (documents); Resident.
Cape Town, 82, 114, 118
Captaincies, *see* Campbell Captaincy; Griquatown Captaincy; Philippolis Captaincy
carpenter's tools, 40
carpentry, 120, 121
Casalis, Eugène, 77, 79 n35, 80
catechetical instruction, 42–43, 45, 48, 71
cattle farming, 29, 31, 42; statistics, 63, 64 n66
cattle raiding, 24–26, 27 n9, 47 n26, 77 n25; expedition against Mzilikazi (1831), 77, 85. *See also* Bergenaars; Bushmen:cattle raiding.
censorship of reports (LMS), *see* editing and censorship of reports
censure (religious), 91
censuses, *see* statistics (general)
children, 70, 71. *See also* Bushmen: children; education (general); sale of children; schoolchildren; schools.
church associations, *see* Auxiliary Mission Society; maternal association; temperance movement
church attendance, 32, 38, 41–42, 45, 48, 59, 63, 68–69 *passim*, 72, 73 *passim*, 80, 82, 102, 107, 121, 121–122
church building, 17, 38, 40, 43, 59, 63, 78, 66, 67, 84; temporary ex-

134

tension, 66: uncompleted building (1827), 38, 41 n10; new building begun (1827), 46, 48; in use, 70; description, 70
church discipline, 69, 91, 111
church government, 69
church membership, 72–73, 87–88; admissions, 70, 78, 111; statistics, 78, 80–82 *passim*, 84, 107. *See also* candidates for baptism and church membership; church attendance.
church music, *see* hymns
church services, 38, 66, 78 *passim*, 82, 107, 109. *See also* communion (celebration).
civil war (1838), 104–105
Clark, James, 15–21 *passim*, 26, 84; use of Dutch, 16; and establishment of Griquas at Philippolis, 22–35 *passim*; proposed 'Captain' of Baster community, 32–33
clay floors, 120
clothing (traditional), 39, 56
clothing (western), 39
Colesberg, 11 n2, 76, 76, 97, 99, 125
Colesberg district, 69 n8, 105
collections and subscriptions, 64, 67, 81, 118
coloured population (general): in mission field, 9–21 *passim*. *See also* Baster community (Philippolis); Griquas; Khoikhoi; 'native teachers'; 'Oorlams'.
commandoes, 40, 44–45, 70, 71
Commercial Advertiser (newspaper), 99 n64
communion (celebration), 66, 68, 73, 79, 111
congregation (Philippolis): criticised by P. Wright, 98. *See also* baptisms; burials; candidates for baptism and church membership; collections and subscriptions; marriages; religious life (personal); *and headings beginning with* church...
Constabel, Andries, 16
Constabel family, 14

conversion (personal), *see* religious life (personal)
conversions to Christianity: first Tswana baptisms, 123. *See also* candidates for baptism and church membership; church membership: admissions.
corn lands, *see* wheat farming
Corner, W.F., 10
corporal punishment, 40–41
Council (executive body), *see* Raad
cultivated land, 59

dairy farming, 31
dams, 50
dancing (traditional), 42
David (teacher), 10
Davids, Anna, 17, 18
Davidson, ?, (Philippolis), 87–88, 90
Davidson, Adam, 89 n47
Davidson, Alexander, 89 n47
day of prayer and humiliation, 68
day schools, *see* schools
de Bruin, Joseph, 73–74
de Bruyn, Katrina, 17, 18
deacons, *see* church government
Demerara, 10
'Diedrik' (coloured man), *see* Vlermuis, Diederik
Difaqane, 27 n9, 51 n37
Dithakong, *see* Lattakoo (mission)
Douglas, 55 n44
Drakensberg, 51 n37
dress, *see* clothing
Driefontein, 71 n12, 121
drinking, *see* intemperance; liquor trade
droughts, 52, 59, 119
drunkenness, *see* intemperance
Dutch language, 15 n16, 16, 43 n20, 44, 51, 77, 78, 110, 111, 123; quoted, 13, 14, 17–18; hymnal, 78; hymns, 75; religious tracts, 57

Edenburg, 113 n11, 117 n25
editing and censorship of reports (LMS), 16, 57, 58, 75 n21, 79, 113 n8; examples, 113–115 *passim*

135

education (general), 40, 52, 53, 54, 55, 74, 101, 115. *See also* infant schools; literacy; monitor system (schools); schools.
elders, *see* church government
English language, 78
epidemics, *see* smallpox
evangelisation, *see entries beginning mission to*...; *also the subheading* evangelisation *under names of specific groups, and references under* pastoral work
evangelists (coloured), *see* coloured population (general):in mission field; native agents; 'native teachers'
exclusion from church, 91, 111
excommunication, *see* exclusion from church

factions (Philippolis), *see* Baster community; 'Griqua party'
Fairbairn, John, 99
farmers (white), *see* Boers
farming, 31. *See also* barley cultivation; cattle farming; dairy farming; gardens; irrigation; sheep farming; tobacco cultivation; wheat farming.
farming implements, *see* ploughs
fasting (penance), 68
Faure, Abraham, 10, 11 n5, 17, 21, 53 n41
field cornets (Cape Colony), 57, 68, 73
Flermuis (surname), *see* Vlermuis
fords (Orange River), 15 n19
fountains, 19, 20, 23, 27, 31, 37, 46, 74, 113, 117; Philippolis, 37, 41, 58; statistics, 59. *See also* water supply.
Fraserburg, 9
Freeman, J.J., 82, 90, 108; and allegations against G.A. Kolbe, 83, 85, 86, 90
French missionaries, *see* Paris Missionary Society
Frontier Wars, 83 n40, 86
fruit trees, 59; statistics, 64

game, 11, 74. *See also* hunting expeditions.
gardens, 17, 19, 37, 63; mission garden, 108, 111; statistics, 59, 63. *See also* irrigation.
Gebel, August, 76
German language, 77
German missionaries, *see* Berlin Missionary Society
Gill, William, 29
glass windows, 111, 120
Goeyman, Elizabeth (Betta), *see* Wiese, Elizabeth (Betta) (Goeyman)
Goeyman, Jan, 10–21 *passim*, 36, 38, 76, 104, 125 n46; command of Dutch, 15 n16; praised, 12; sister, 17 n27; wife, 18 *passim*, 20 *passim*
Gosport (England), 11 n5
Gosselin, Constant, 79 n35, 80
Government Agent (Griquatown), 32, 44, 60–62 *passim*
government (Philippolis Captaincy), *see* Raad (Philippolis)
Graaff-Reinet, 10(2x), 18, 21, 30, 33, 46, 83 n41, 85, 99; mission work, 65, 84
Graaff-Reinet district, 52
Graaff-Reinet Missionary Society, 65 n1
Graham's Town, 72, 86
grass huts, *see* mat huts
Gregorowski, Reinhold, 75
Griqua Country (term), 24
'Griqua party' (Philippolis): opposition to J. Melvill, 43–44, 46–48, 60–62; opposition to G.A. Kolbe, 71, 84–86, 105. *See also* Hendrickze, Hendrik.
Griquas, 22; dress, 39; language, 111 n4; women, 39; and early mission, 11; evangelisation, 40; criticised, 39–40. *See also* Bergenaars; Campbell Captaincy; Griquatown Captaincy; Philippolis Captaincy.
Griquatown (mission), 10, 19, 22, 32, 45, 46, 94. *See also* Government Agent (Griquatown),
Griquatown Captaincy, 13, 22, 97;

Raad, 73
Grootfontein, 49
gunpowder, *see* arms and ammunition

Hankey, 16, 62
Hans (Bushman), 24
Hardcastle, 55 n44
hartbeeshuis, 12
Hendrickze, Hendrik, 15 n19, 47, 59 n54, 77, 84–86; as interpreter, 78; religious life, 48–49; opposition to G.A. Kolbe, 84–86, 104, 105
Hendriks, Andries, 14
Hephzibah, 10, 12
Hodgson, T.L., 12, 51 n39
Hopetown, 11 n3
horses, 117; statistics, 63
'Hottentot' (term), 13 n14. *See further* Baster community (Philippolis); Griquas; Khoikhoi.
Hough, Messrs., (Algoa Bay), 112
houses (general), 27, 30, 34. *See also* clay floors; glass windows; hartbeeshuis; mat huts; mission house; Philippolis:number of houses; thatch roofs.
Hoxton (England), 125 n45
hunting expeditions, 53, 54, 77
huts, *see* mat huts
hymnal, 78
hymns, 70, 75, 78

illiteracy, *see under* literacy
illness, 118, 123. *See also* smallpox.
infant schools, 81, 82, 84, 122–123
infanticide, 55
'institution' (term), 9 n1
intemperance, 72, 74, 81, 85 *passim*, 102. *See also* liquor trade; temperance society.
interpreters, 14, 42, 45, 50, 53, 56, 78, 109–110, 113, 117
irrigation, 31, 50, 59
itinerating (cattle farmers), 31, 37, 42, 56, 64, 74–75
itinerating (missionaries), 37, 49–50, 56, 58; journals, 50–58, 112–118
itinerating (schoolteachers), 21

Jenkins, Thomas, 68, 69
Joris (Bushman kaptyn), 41 (name not mentioned), 42
Joubert, Gideon, 68, 73

Kalkfontein, 50, 54, 57
karosses, 56
Kat River, 86, 120
Khoi community (Philippolis), *see* Baster community
Khoi languages (general), 78, 110. *See also* Xiri (language).
Khoikhoi, 10; criticised 41–42. *See also* Baster community (Philippolis); Griquas.
Kicherer, J.J., 9, 10
Klaarwater (mission), *see* Griquatown
'Klein Hendrik', *see* Hendrickze, Hendrik
Kok, Abraham, 93 n52, 101 n66, 103–104
Kok, Adam, II, 32, 42, 46, 58, 85 *passim*, 86, 89 n49; establishment at Philippolis, 22–35 *passim*; number of followers, 28; and mission, 40, 44, 47–48, 60–61; religious life, 48, 55, 57; wealth, 77; proposed gift from LMS, 40; wife, 59 n54, 60, 121 n41; son (unidentified), 43; death, 82
Kok, Adam, III, 121
Kok, Cornelius, II, 89, 102
Kok, Cornelius, III, 43 n17, 47, 50; widow, 59 n54
Kok, Fortuin, 60
Kolbe, G.A., 35, 64 n66, 65–105; early life, 65, 77, 84; appointment to Philippolis, 62, 65–66; ordination, 79–80; salary, 65, 89; description, 77; opposition by 'Griqua party', 71, 84–86; trading activities, 89, 95, 96, 99, 102, 105; farms, 71 n12, 91, 95, 101, 105, 121; other property, 99, 108;
  alleged adultery, 82–105 *passim*; banished from Captaincy, 95–99 *passim*; criticised by P. Wright, 98–103 *passim*; resignation, 91, 92, 95,

137

101, 108; after resignation, 95–96, 101, 105, 121; family, 65, 85, 87, 89(2x), 92, 96, 104, 105; death, 105
Kolbe, Margaret, 65, 65–66, 83, 85, 105; marital problems, 87–89, 93, 100, 104–105
Koningfontein, 10–11
Konnah (mission station), 10, 12
Konstabel family, see Constabel family
Kora language, 78
Korana, 34, 50; dress, 39; evangelisation, 39, 50–54, 53–54, 54, 67, 71, 76, 78, 93, 116–117; statistics, 38, 39
kraals (settlements), see werfs
Kraut, G.A., 78
Krotz, Adam, 24
Kruger, Abraham, 53
Kruisman (teacher), 10
Kuruman (mission), 45 n23, 105 n70

L.M.S., see London Missionary Society
Lancaster system (schools), see British system
Lattakoo (mission), 10, 11, 37 n5, 45–46. See also Kuruman.
Lemue, Eléonore, 79 n35
Lemue, Prosper, 79 n35, 80
Lephoi (Tlhaping Chief), 76
liquor trade, 72, 74
literacy, 39 n8, 48, 76, 98, 107, 110, 117. See also education (general); school materials; schools.
local preachers, 125 n46
locusts, 63, 81, 114, 119
London Missionary Society (LMS), 9; missionary college, 11 n5, 124; Missionary Communion, 114–115; editing and censorship of missionary reports, 16, 57, 58, 75 n21, 79; agent (Cape Town), 49; and defence of Northern frontier, 22, 62, 65 104–105, 126; praised, 78. See also Auxiliary Mission Society; mission to Bushmen; Philip, John.

Lord's Supper, see communion
Lückhoff, 13

'maatskap' (relationship), 42
Madagascar, 106
Malmesbury, 29 n19
Mantatees, see Tlkowa tribe
Maropeng, 10–11
marriages, 81, 118
Martyn, Henry, 78
massacre (Boesmansfontein), 23–26 passim
mat huts, 42, 43 n19, 54, 114
Matabeles (amaNdebele), see Ndebele tribe
Matabeles (Transorange), 50
maternal association, 111
Maurits, Martha, see Pretorius, Martha (Maurits)
medical services, 73, 118. See also vaccination.
medical supplies, 112, 118, 123
Melvill, Anna Frederica (Stadler), 36, 49, 64
Melvill, John, 32, 36–64 passim; arrival at Philippolis, 36; correspondence with London, 36; opposition from 'Griqua party', 43–44, 46–48, 60–62; support of Baster community, 46–47; family, 36, 64; farm, 71 n12, 91, 121 n41; removal from station, 62
Mfecane, see Difaqane
Miles, Richard, (missionary), 24, 46, 59–60, 62, 65, 84, 115 n16
Miles, Richard, (Tswana convert), 114
mission farm, 25, 119
mission garden, 108, 111
mission house, 12, 20, 38, 46, 59; 'old mission house', 123; temporary accommodation, 108–109; new building (1836), 108, 111–112, 119–120, 124; description and plans, 108, 121 n38
mission to Bushmen: 9–20 passim, 42, 45; mission at Philippolis, 12, 32; criticised, 26–27, 27–29, 31–32; and settlement of Griquas, 25, 26,

138

28; projected removal, 23, 27, 30, 33; removed to Caledon River, 35; later settlement on station, 41, 42, 55, 57; gift of cattle, 55, 57; school attendance, 56; abandonment of Bushman mission, 76
mission to Korana, *see* Korana:evangelisation
mission to Madagascar, 106
mission to slaves, 65
mission to Sotho people, 76, 79 n35
mission to Tswana, *see* Tswana people:evangelisation
mission work (general), 45–46; by coloured people, 9–21 *passim*. *See also the references under* pastoral work.
missionaries, 124; college (LMS), 11 n5, 124; ordination (G.A. Kolbe), 79–80; salaries, 65: rivalry between Griquatown and Kuruman, 45 n23; accusations of adultery, 104, 105 n70
Missionary Communion (LMS), 114–115
missionary prayer meetings, 38, 66, 68, 111
Modder River: as name for Lower Riet River, 23 n2
Moffat, Robert, 11, 45–56, 105 n70, 125 n46
monitor system (schools), 111 n5
Monro, John, 86
Moshweshwe (Sotho Chief), 76
Mothito (mission), 79 n35
Murray, Andrew, Sr., 52, 65 n1
Mzilikazi (Ndebele chief), 22, 51 n37, 77, 85
Namaqualand, 50, 51

native agents (LMS), 125 n46
'native teachers', 124–125
Ndebele tribe, 22, 51 n37, 77 n25
New Hantam, 69 n8
Northern frontier, 22, 62, 65 104–105, 126
Norval's Pont, 83 n41

'Old Inhabitants' (Philippolis), *see* Baster community (Philippolis)
Old Philip (Kora), *see* Philip
'Oorlams' (term), 28, 29 n15, 49
Orange River ('Zwart River'), 15 n22, 52, 53, 97
ordinations (G.A. Kolbe), 79–80

painting (personal adornment), 39
paper, 112
Paris Missionary Society, 76, 76, 79–80, 125 n46; and allegations against G.A. Kolbe, 83, 85–86 *passim*, 88, 96, 100
passes (documents), 14, 30, 37
pastoral work, *see entries and references under* Bible study; catechetical work; church associations; church services; congregation (Philippolis); itinerating (missionaries); missionary prayer meetings; prayer meetings; Sabbath school
Peel, ?, (Wesleyan), 72–73
Pellissier, J.P., 79 n35, 80, 96, 102, 105 n70
Pellissier, Martha, 79 n35
personal religion, *see* religious life (personal)
Petrusburg, 117 n25
Petrusville, 11 n2
Philip (Kora), 54
Philip, Jane, 92, 108
Philip, John, 10, 13, 76, 82; in Transorange (1825) 14–16, 37, 53 n43; and establishment of Philippolis Captaincy, 22–35 *passim*; and J. Goeyman & J. Clark, 17–20 *passim*; and J. Melvill, 62; and G.A. Kolbe, 84, 86, 91, 93, 99, 105; and T. Atkinson, 106, 108, 122–126 *passim*; plans for Northern Frontier, 22, 62, 65, 104–105, 126
Philippolis (mission and village): establishment, 12; name, 13; original owner of fountain, 41; made over to Griquas, 22–35 *passim*, 38; general surveys and reports, (1827–35) 37–40, 59, 63–64, 79, 80–82,

139

(1836) 107–109; census (1831), 63–64; descriptions, 76–79; unstable population, 37, 49, 59, 64, 107, 121; number of houses, 38, 59, 77; temporary removal of settlement, 46, 49, 58, 60; need for second missionary, 107–108, 118, 121; same appointed, 124, 125.
See further under specific headings, e.g. church building; congregation; population figures; water supply. *See also* mission to Bushmen.
Philippolis Captaincy: establishment, 10, 12, 17, 22–35 *passim*, 38; area, 63; proposed migration, 92. *See also* Baster community (Philippolis); civil war (1838); 'Griqua party' (Philippolis); Kok, Adam, II; population figures; Raad (Philippolis); treaties.
ploughing and sowing, *see* gardens; wheat farming
ploughs, 18, 19; statistics, 63, 64 n66
Pniel (mission), 95 n56
population figures: Philippolis (village), 37–38, 63, 107; Philippolis Captaincy, 28, 38, 39, 59, 63, 80; fighting men, 77;
Port Elizabeth, 122–123. *See also* Algoa Bay.
prayer meetings, 38, 55–56, 57, 69, 70, 71, 107. *See also* missionary prayer meetings.
preaching, *see* church services; interpreters; itinerating (missionaries)
Pretorius, Andries, Jr., 29 n16, 30
Pretorius, Andries, Sr., 10, 11 n7, 28–29 *passim*, 32–33, 41
Pretorius, Martha (Maurits), 41 n12
public worship, *see* church services
punishments, 40–41, 70
punitive expeditions, *see* commandoes

Raad (Griquatown), 73
Raad (Philippolis), 49, 58, 74, 97–98, 126; and G.A, Kolbe, 85, 90, 95–101 *passim*

raiding parties, *see* Bergenaars; Bushmen:cattle raiding; cattle raiding
Ramah (mission), 10–13 *passim*, 50, 51 n38
Read, James, 10, 11, 26, 29 n16, 37 n5
reading and writing, *see* education (general); literacy; schools
reading matter, 57, 76, 82. *See also* Bibles; religious tracts.
reception of church members, *see* candidates for baptism and church membership; church membership
reed huts, *see* mat huts
refugees, *see* Sotho-Tswana refugees; Tlhaping tribe:refugees
Regshande (Korana), 76
religious conversion, *see* conversion to Christianity; religious life (personal)
religious instruction, 122. *See also* Bible study; candidates for baptism and church membership; catechetical instruction; itinerating (missionaries); Sabbath school; *and references under* pastoral work.
religious life (personal), 41, 48–49, 50–52, 52, 54, 55–56 *passim*, 66–74 *passim*, 122. *See also* conversions to Christianity; prayer meetings; revivals (religious).
religious tracts, 57, 81, 82, 113–118 *passim*
Resident (Transgariep), 87 n46
revivals (religious), 47 n24, 66–74 *passim*
Riet River, 22, 23, 28, 53 n43, 76
Right Hand Korana, 76
Robertson, ?, (Graaff-Reinet), 25
Rondefontein, 114

Sabba, Piet, 10, 50, 53, 58, 75–76
Sabbath observance, 30, 43
Sabbath school, 107, 110
Sak River, 9. *See also* Zak River (mission).
sale of children, 42
Schalkwyk, Ockert, *see* van Schalk-

wyk, Ockert
Schietfontein, 117
school attendance, 38, 49, 56, 59, 66(2x), 68, 70, 81, 82, 110, 121
school building, 38, 49, 84; new building, 110, 119, 122, 123 n44, 125
school materials, 48, 76, 112, 114–116 *passim*
'school place' (term), 9 n1
school teachers, 21, 76, 114, 116, 122–123
schoolchildren, 18, 20
schools, 38, 101, 107 *passim*, 110, 112–113; system of instruction, 110; in district, 21, 114; statistics, 32. See also education (general); infant schools; literacy.
Schreiner, Gottlob, 123 n44, 125–126
Schreiner, Rebecca (Lyndall), 125
sermons, *see* church services; itinerating (missionaries)
Setswana (language), *see* Tswana language
settlements, *see* werfs
sewing school, 49
sheep farming: statististics, 63, 64 n66
sheet lessons (schools), *see* school materials
shopkeeping, 89, 102
sickness, 118, 123. See also smallpox.
singing, *see* hymns
Skietfontein, 117
slates (writing materials), 48
slave trade, 30. See also sale of children.
slaves, 65
smallpox, 69, 71; vaccination, 68
Smit, Erasmus, 10(2x)
Smith, Andrew, 26, 76, 83 n41
societies, *see* church associations
Somerset East, 29 n19
Sotho people, 38, 76, 79 n35
Sotho-Tswana refugees (general), 15 n18, 37–38, 50. See also 'Caffres' (generic term); Sotho people; Tswana tribe.
South African Commercial Advertiser
(newspaper), 99 n64
sowing and ploughing, *see* gardens; wheat farming
spelling books, *see* school materials
Springbok Korana, 95 n56
Springfontein, 115
springs, *see* fountains
Stadler, Anna Frederica, *see* Melvill, Anna Frederica (Stadler)
statistics (general), 63–64. See also church attendance; population figures; school attendance; *and under specific subjects, e.g.* cattle farming; church membership; fruit trees; Tswana people; wagons.
Stockenstrom, Andries, 13, 23, 34, 35, 55 n46, 97–98, 98–99
Stoffels, Andries, 16
subscriptions, *see* collections and subscriptions
Sunday school, *see* Sabbath school
Sutton, William, 87

Tambookies, *see* Thembu people
teachers, *see* school teachers
temperance society, 73–74, 81
tents, 53, 66
testimonies (religious), *see* religious life (personal)
thatch roofs, 43, 119, 120, 122
Thembu people, 51 n37
timber, 108, 111, 120–121 *passim*
Tlhaping tribe, 10; refugees, 76
Tlokwa tribe ('Mantatees'), 56, 57 n50
tobacco, 87
tobacco cultivation, 31
Toomfontein, 113
Toornberg, 10–11 *passim*, 12
tracts, *see* religious tracts
traders, 98
trading and barter, 14, 29, 89. See also Kolbe, G.A.:trading activities; liquor trade; sale of children; shopkeeping.
transport, 118, 119–120
treaties, 82, 94, 97–98, 104
Trompsburg, 113 n11

Tswana language, 110
Tswana people, 42, 67, 125–126; in service of Korana, 54; dancing, 42; evangelisation, 39, 45, 56, 57, 73, 107, 109, 110, 111, 113, 117, 118, 123–125 *passim*; converts, 114; first baptisms, 123; school attendance, 38, 56; statistics, 37–38, 39, 49, 59, 109–110. *See also* Sotho-Tswana refugees (general).

Uitkomst, 116

vaccination, 68
van Schalkwyk, Ockert, 72
vegetable gardens, *see* gardens
visitation (pastoral), *see* itinerating (missionaries)
Vlermuis, Diederik, 50–52, 52, 54
Vlermuis, Kobus, 50, 51 n39

wagons, 70, 87, 113, 117; statistics, 63, 64 n66
water supply, 15, 19–20, 37, 49 *passim*, 58. *See also* fountains; irrigation.
Waterboer, Andries, 22, 73, 82, 94, 97
weddings, *see* marriages
werfs (settlements), 50, 51, 53, 75; definition, 51 n36; 'kraals' (usage of T. Atkinson), 113–117 *passim*
Wesleyan Missionary Society, 125 n46, 126

wheat farming, 11, 18, 19, 20, 23, 31, 63, 117, 119
white farmers, *see* Boers
Wiese, Andries, 83, 87, 89(2x), 92, 98, 105
Wiese, Elizabeth (Betta) (Goeyman), 83, 85, 87, 88–89, 101
windows, *see* glass windows
Witbooi, Mietje. 17, 18
women: religious life, 41, 54, 55–56; Bible study, 110; maternal association, 111; school teachers, 116, 122–123; dress (traditional), 39. *See also* Atkinson, Henrietta Elizabeth (Arderne); Kolbe, Margaret.
Wright, Peter, 22, 33, 104; appointment to Philippolis, 126; and allegations against G.A. Kolbe, 88, 94–105 *passim*
writing and reading, *see* literacy
writing paper, 112
wykmeester (official), 83 n41

Xhosa people, 25–26. *See also* 'Caffres' (generic term).
Xiri (language), 111 n4

Yzerbek, Goliat, 76

Zak River (mission), 9, 10(2x)
Zuid-Afrikaan (newspaper), 99
'Zwart River', *see* Orange River